D0599611

ENDANGERED ENVIRONMENTS

SAVING THE EARTH'S VANISHING ECOSYSTEMS

Anna Maria Caldara

MALLARD PRESS
An imprint of BDD Promotional Book Company, Inc.
666 Fifth Avenue
New York, NY 10103

The cleaner our oceans, the healthier the wildlife that depends on them.

© Rob Mustard

One of the basic values of this book is its clarity in presenting the consequences of our present activities on the biosystems of the planet and the urgent need to deal with these addictions. This altering of our conduct has three phases: increasing our awareness of the impending disaster, cessation of our harmful activities, and healing the damage already done. These are universal obligations. Everyone can contribute to these efforts to ensure the survival of the planet, and thereby give ourselves and our children a context for continued human existence.

We can take much encouragement from certain events of recent years. Through the work of World Watch and of the World Resource Institute we have attained a new clarity as regards our present situation. The media has raised environmental issues. The shock needed to bring about a recovery is now being felt throughout all levels of society. The consciousness of danger now exists, the rate of devastation begins to diminish, the healing is begun.

In 1984 it was estimated by Lester Milbraith that there were some 12,000 associations, movements, periodicals, and newsletters dedicated to the environment. From the number of notices and new publications flowing across my desk since then, I would guess that there must be nearly twice that number at the present time.

The Director of the United Nations has recently stated that the issue of the environment is at the top of the international agenda, and it was the foremost concern at the last meeting of the Organization for Economic Cooperation and Development. A major celebration is planned for 1992 in relation to the twentieth anniversary of the Stockholm Conference, the first of the major international conferences on the environment. Whereas prior to this conference there were no environmental protection agencies in our governments, the delegates went home from this conference and established such agencies in almost ninety percent of the nations that attended.

Garbage is graded at a landfill in Salt Lake City, Utah, while seagulls hunt in the pile for food.

© Gary Crandall/Envision

From all these and a multitude of other events that have taken place we can conclude that a pervasive consciousness now exists of the plight of the planet. We now recognize that a thousand things need to be done, all the way from recycling our paper and our metal containers to completely transforming our lifestyles, especially by reducing our use of (and possibly eliminating) the gas-driven automobile.

Beyond all the particular things that need to be done there is a general need to transform our basic values. This applies especially to our religious and educational establishments, which have been terribly negligent in dealing with this situation. Our religious institutions have long ago developed ways of dealing morally with such issues as suicide, homicide, and genocide; yet they are totally lacking in moral principles for dealing with biocide and geocide—evils at least as disastrous.

So too with education. We educate our children for efficiency in running our commercial-industrial institutions, precisely those establishments that are tearing the planet to pieces and saturating it with toxic wastes, especially the petrochemical industries. Even though we have developed organic agriculture to a newly efficient degree, our universities continue to teach reliance on chemical-based agriculture. Similarly, despite the vast amounts of toxic waste from our nuclear industry that we cannot dispose of, we remain negligent in committing our energies and our finances toward the development of solar energy. We are still not giving our students basic information on the dangers of fossil fuels and the destruction of our forests in building up the blanket of greenhouse gases in the atmosphere.

Everyone can make a significant contribution. We must begin to recognize the dangers of a consumer society. We can revise our lifestyles to reflect the needs and activities of the planet itself.

This pasture rose* (Rosa carolina) *blooms amid a refuse heap, determined to brighten the landscape.

There was a time, prior to our use of the automobile and the development of the petrochemical industry, when we did not need to know a great deal about the earth or how it functioned in relation to our human activities. That is no longer true. Today all of us urgently need to know the implications of using polystyrene cups, dishes, or fillers, or plastic linings for diapers. As automobile owners we need to know that each year we put an amount of carbon dioxide into the atmosphere equal to the weight of the car itself.

By identifying so many of the specific forms of our present situation the author not only clarifies the realities of our present situation but offers specific remedies that can be applied to the issues. She brings the issue before us not only in its urgency but also with directions as to how we can meet the difficulty. While there is no single answer to the problem, the suggestions given here will work for almost everyone.

Read this book and you will no longer live in deadly innocence, nor will you feel so frustrated as to what you can do with your knowledge. The people of Los Angeles that I mentioned at the beginning of this introduction have already committed themselves to severely limiting their polluting activities. If these people can become aware of their situation and commit themselves to change it, then the rest of us should be able to rethink our present condition and proceed with the radical transformations that are needed.

Thomas Berry,
Director, Riverdale Center for Earth Studies
Riverdale, New York

The Ozone Layer

Brightening the abyss of space as it spins in a mass of swirling colors is the earth. Beyond the ashen craters of the moon rises our planet, its surface a marbled canvas of blue and white.

A delicate "skin" of water and gases envelops the earth. This moist cushion extends from the deepest point of the ocean floor to the outer reaches of the atmosphere, several hundred miles above the ground. The water, air, and soil systems of the globe work together to sustain life, and to renew and purify themselves. A constant recycling of the chemical elements necessary for life—water, minerals, oxygen, phosphorus, and carbon, among others—must take place, because no new elements enter or leave the ecosphere.

The ozone layer is a fragile swath of gas that absorbs almost all of the harmful ultraviolet (UV) radiation emanating from the sun. It shields our planet like a blanket. Found in its densest concentrations at altitudes ranging from 7 to 15 miles (12 to 25 km) above the earth, the ozone layer is only a few parts per million thick. Indeed, if *all* of the ozone in the stratosphere, a region 12 to 31 miles (20 to 50 km) high, were condensed to our own atmospheric pressure, our precious ozone layer would be but the width of a dime.

Why should the condition of a canopy of molecules far above the globe concern us? The answer is that the ozone layer is a vital link among the physical components necessary to sustain life on Earth. A damaged ozone layer allows lethal ultraviolet radiation to reach the planet. The effects of that radiation will be manifested in higher incidences of skin cancer, wide-scale depression of immune systems, increased levels of smog, lower crop yields, and deterioration of marine harvests. Perhaps even more significant than these sobering predictions is the relationship between ozone depletion and global warming, and the destruction of the ocean's *phytoplankton*, the organisms that form the very basis of the food chain.

A documented hole in the ozone layer exists. It materializes over Antarctica each September, and scientists have noted that it has worsened each year since 1979. In the late 1980s, the gap was two times the size of the continental United States. Scientific opinion varies on the reason why the hole keeps reappearing. The reason why it exists at all, however, is clear: It can largely be blamed on the presence of chlorofluorocarbons (CFCs) in the atmosphere.

Ozone losses have been documented in other areas of the world as well. An average yearly loss of three percent of ozone has been noticed above Arosa, Switzerland, for at least 10 years. Seven hundred miles (1100 km) from the North Pole, over Spitzbergen, Norway, a hole one-third the size of Antarctica's has been pinpointed.

A NASA international research team that recently completed a study of the arctic atmosphere's chemical composition had more to announce: The conditions needed for ozone depletion were present over the Arctic as well. Cold winter air, trapped above the poles for weeks, combines with icy clouds, sunlight, and chemically active CFCs in a way that speeds ozone destruction.

A prominent drop in ozone has been verified at three out of five Australian ozone-monitoring locations. Whether or not the loss was due to the Antarctic depletion stretching over Australia is still unknown.

Courtesy NASA

Left: ***This splendid view of Earth, from the Mediterranean Sea area to Antarctica's south polar ice cap, was photographed from the*** **Apollo 17** ***spacecraft.*** **Above:** ***Polar stratospheric clouds photographed at almost 39,000 feet (11,700 m) north of Stavanger, Norway. These "Type II" clouds consist mostly of water molecules frozen as ice.***

Courtesy NASA

THE IMPACT OF CFCs

CFCs are found most commonly as the propellant in spray cans, coolant in refrigerators and air conditioners, in foam and plastic insulation, and in industrial solvents. Widespread agreement exists in the scientific community that Antarctica's ozone loss is triggered by chlorine, from the use of CFCs, and bromine, a component of fire retardants.

What is it about CFCs that makes them so perilous to the ozone layer? The CFC class of molecules, ironically, was developed by industrial chemists who were seeking a non-poisonous, non-flammable substance—one that would "safely" propel deodorant out of a can, for example. These molecules are comprised of one or more carbon atoms, to which are attached chlorine and/or fluorine atoms. When the spray button on a can is pushed, the molecules enter the air, bounce off

It's easy to push a spray button on an aerosol can, but this simple action releases hordes of CFCs into the atmosphere. **Right:** ***Styrofoam products, made with CFCs, pose a major threat to the environment. So many different applications for Styrofoam and CFCs have been found that their use continues worldwide, although many local communities are instituting programs to ban Styrofoam products.***

© Ken Graham

the walls and eventually find their way outside—a journey that may take days or weeks. Continuing to ricochet off trees and telephone poles, the CFCs are lifted by wind currents and they "fly" ever upwards. Several years later, they arrive in the high atmosphere, most without having broken down or combined chemicallv with any other molecules along the way.

In that high atmosphere, where ozone prevails, a CFC molecule will remain for a century before it surrenders its chlorine. The chlorine, upon encountering the ozone molecule, destroys it—without destroying itself. And therein lies the truly frightening nature of the CFC: It will take years before the chlorine reenters the lower atmosphere and is removed via rainwater. During that time, one atom of chlorine can demolish 100,000 molecules of ozone!

It was in 1973 that atmospheric chemists F. Sherwood Rowland and Mario Molina of the University of California at Irvine postulated the connection between ozone depletion and CFCs. When their report appeared in the June 1974 issue of *Nature*, shock waves reverberated through the $3-billion-a-year fluorocarbon industry. How could a product that had contributed so much to the ease of modern life be exposed as a hazard to populations worldwide?

Dozens of applications for CFCs had been discovered during the World War II era. "Freon," the trademark for CFC-12, became an internationally popular refrigeration coolant. Production increased by 4,000 percent between 1931 and 1945. Aerosol propellants against malaria were made with CFCs 11 and 12 during the war; afterwards, hair spray and softer carpet pads, sofa and auto cushions all evolved from the wonders of CFCs. From 1945 to 1950, the total production of CFCs doubled when Dow Chemical Company began manufacturing Styrofoam.

As a result of the energy crisis of the 1970s, homeowners and businesspeople began looking for more efficient means of heating and insulating their residences. The fabrication of rigid foam insulation, blown with CFC-11 and CFC-12, skyrocketed. In 1985, two-thirds of the insulation placed in new commercial buildings in the United States was rigid foam, as was half of the insulation in new, single-family homes, and a third of the entire home re-insulation market.

Today, shoppers strolling the aisles of giant malls and employees working in skyscrapers are kept comfortable by enormous chilling units that utilize CFCs. Families are more inclined to travel in the summer, because 80 percent of the cars sold in the United States are equipped with air conditioners. The scope of CFC use even extends to the food we buy in the supermarket. Three-fourths of the American diet is refrigerated at some point before it is consumed.

The versatility of the CFC family of chemicals explains why they have pervaded our culture so thoroughly. The fastest-growing CFC in use worldwide is number 113. It can clean computer microchips as well as clothes that would normally be subjected to more immediately toxic dry-cleaning solutions. As a solvent, it also removes grease, glue, and dried solder from metals and plastics.

An organization of the CFC industry itself, The Alliance for Responsible CFC Policy, places the value of the annual production of these chemicals in the U.S. alone plus the materials and services directly dependent on them at $135 billion.

OZONE DEPLETION AND HEALTH

On a personal level, who hasn't sighed gratefully when cooled by an air conditioner on a hot day? But evidence is mounting that this CFC-based form of relief has a hidden cost: our health. Illness is directly related to the ozone layer's decline.

The NASA Ozone Trends Panel reported on the efforts of more than 100 scientists who spent almost a year and a half re-analyzing every bit of information collected from satellite and ground-based ozone data. Their conclusions? 1. The hole in the layer over Antarctica was caused by the presence of CFCs. 2. The poles are not the only places where ozone is missing; losses are occurring around the planet. 3. Ozone has consistently decreased by over one-and-a-half to three percent in the last 20 years, in the area where most of the world's population lives. The decreases were most noticeable in the winter, depending on latitude.

NASA further reports that the ozone layer has already declined more than two percent on a global scale. It is proceeding to degenerate far more rapidly than computer models have anticipated. Moreover, a further deterioration is imminent; tons of chemicals still being released into the atmosphere have not yet reached the ozone layer.

The effects of increased amounts of UV radiation on bacteria, soil, and mammals are not well-known. However, it is known that increased exposure in humans can bring about a surge in skin cancers and an impairment of the body's immune system. Light-skinned peoples are most vulnerable to the threat of skin cancers. Scientist Carl Sagan has already written that light-skinned people may need to wear protective clothing and strong sun-block ointments just to perform ordinary outdoor tasks.

World Watch Institute reports that each year, the two most common forms of skin cancer, squamous cell and basal cell carcinoma, attack 600,000 people in the United States. The number of victims worldwide is three times *higher*. These cancers have been attributed to skin changes caused by cumulative exposure to UV radiation.

Melanoma, a form of skin cancer that causes the most fatalities, is connected with extreme UV radiation exposure, as in cases of severe sunburn. It is responsible for more than half of all skin cancer deaths. Frighteningly, incidences of melanoma have sharply increased around the world within the last few years.

The AIDS virus has demonstrated all too well the inability of damaged immune systems to cope with the ravages of opportunistic disease. In the scenario of ozone depletion, increased exposure to UV-B rays (wave lengths that inflict the most biological harm on humans, animals, and plants) is expected to lower the body's resistance to invading organisms. Although a jump in skin cancers would primarily affect the light-skinned population, an immuno-deficiency caused by degraded ozone could affect virtually every single person on the earth.

The threat to human health from a diminishing layer of high-atmosphere ozone is further complicated by the phenomenon known as "photochemical smog," or ground-level ozone. Stratospheric

ozone guards the earth from the dangerous effects of UV radiation, and is a factor in the balance of worldwide climate. Ground-level ozone is caused when atmospheric air pollutants react with hydrocarbons and nitrogen oxides under the influence of sunlight. (Hydrocarbons, organic compounds containing carbon and hydrogen, emerge from burned or somewhat-burned gasoline. They are also formed in the evaporation of industrial solvents, as from refineries. Nitrogen oxides are pollutants produced by the reaction of nitrogen and oxygen when high temperatures are generated in internal combustion engines and furnaces.) The main component of smog is ground-level ozone. As the high-altitude ozone layer continues to erode, more UV radiation bathes the earth's surface, quickening the photochemical process.

At ground level, ozone is a destructive gas that can burn the inner lining of the lungs. World Resource Institute claims that $4 billion worth of crops are destroyed in the United States every year by ozone at ground level. Some of these crops, such as cotton, soybeans, wheat, and corn, are global staples of clothing and diet. Tree growth is also impaired by the gas. Damage to trees is continuing at a startling rate. It is estimated that half of the trees in many European countries suffer blight from ground-level ozone as well as from acid rain.

The legacy of acid rain—ruined crops, corroded buildings, and gradual deaths of lakes and fish—is enhanced by ground-level ozone. As the upper ozone layer decreases, a greater volume of hydrogen peroxide is believed to collect in the lower atmosphere, where 95 percent of our air exists. Hydrogen peroxide is one of the ingredients capable of producing acid rain.

© Thomas A. Schneider

© Y.R. Tymstra/Valan Photos

Left: ***Emissions of an industrial skyline dim the sunset in Sarnia, Ontario, Canada.*** **Above:** ***Fir trees damaged by acid rain stand decimated in the Great Smoky Mountains National Park, North Carolina.***

© Dave Bartruff/FPG International

THE GREENHOUSE EFFECT

With a weakened ozone layer, the atmosphere is more susceptible to the effects of pollution. The potential for a "global warming" is considered by many scientists to be the most serious environmental problem confronting the human race. A worldwide rise in temperatures could result if a "greenhouse effect" is set in motion. The greenhouse effect begins when CFCs, nitrous oxide, carbon dioxide, and methane are released into the air. Heavier than air, these gases do not dissipate but ring a barrier around the earth. Although sunlight can pass through the barrier and warm the earth, the resulting heat is prevented from flowing back into space. The heat trapped around the earth's surface creates a "greenhouse effect," just as glass traps heat inside a greenhouse. The consequences of such an event would range from heat waves and droughts to the expansion of deserts and the flooding of coastal areas.

Some scientists believe that a greenhouse effect is already occurring. They cite the soaring temperatures and pockets of drought manifested in 1988 as examples of its beginning. Dr. James Hansen, director of NASA's Goddard Institute for Space Studies, stated that the earth was warmer in 1988 than in any other year; the rate of warming in the last 25 years was the highest on record. World Watch Institute noted that in the past century, the five warmest years all occurred in the decade 1980 to 1990.

An understanding of how the greenhouse process was initiated is essential because of global warming's enormous potential repercussions. Why are so many greenhouse gases entering the atmosphere? What factors have combined to start these falling dominoes on their destructive course?

Carbon dioxide levels in the atmosphere began to spiral after 1850, when the smokestacks of the industrial age were erected. Coal, oil, and natural gas were burned more and more frequently, in steadily increasing quantities. Since that time, the combustion of these fuels has risen by one-third.

© R. Weldon/FPG International

Today, a total of 7 billion tons (6 billion metric tons) of carbon dioxide is dispatched into the atmosphere by human activity, most of it from the use of fossil fuels. Deforestation, spurred in poor countries by a self-defeating cycle of land-clearing for cattle and farming, destroys an area of forest each year the size of Belgium. With the loss of forest cover, even more carbon per year is sent skyward. Currently, over one million people who depend on wood for energy are cutting forests faster than they can be replanted. The inevitable outcome, a wood-fuel shortage, could easily occur by the year 2000.

The greenhouse gases unleashed into the air are clearly a reflection of the lifestyles we maintain on Earth. Aerosols still account for a quarter of total CFCs used. Atmospheric concentrations of CFC-11 and CFC-12 are spiraling at five percent per year. Levels of nitrous oxide, loosed in the combustion of coal and the breakdown of agricultural fertilizer, and methane, seeping from landfills, leaking from natural gas pipelines, and being vented in the production of oil, are rising steadily. (Methane is also encountered in flooded soils, such as rice paddies, and is generated in the intestines of cattle and sheep.) These other greenhouse gases are responsible for as much global warming—or more—than carbon dioxide by itself. Approximately 20 other potential greenhouse gases have been identified in addition.

At the present rate of greenhouse gas build-up, the earth becomes .02 to .06 of a degree centigrade warmer each year. Currently, we are feeling the effects of about a 1°F ($\frac{1}{2}$°C) rise in temperature, caused by emissions released before the mid-1980s. It is difficult for scientists to say exactly how much of a future temperature increase will be due to greenhouse gases in the atmosphere. The sensitivity of the earth's climate to even relatively small concentrations of these gases is unknown. If the earth is only partially sensitive, we may see a 3$\frac{1}{2}$°F (2°C) rise. If it is *very* sensitive, we could see a 16°F (9°C) increase. Some scientists believe that significant warming is already unavoidable because of the accumulation of past emissions.

Yet, there has been some progress, albeit minor. Scientists estimate that if CFC production had continued at the same frantic rate as two decades ago, the greenhouse effect today would be much more severe—greater than the impact of carbon dioxide alone. The speed at which the greenhouse effect is proceeding could be controlled if present CFC production was stopped, or at least reduced. Many of the proposed halocarbon substitutes for CFCs contain fluorine, which, although it does not present a specific threat to the ozone layer, nevertheless still contributes to an increased warming of the atmosphere.

The role of the ozone layer in maintaining world climate and in protecting the health of all living things should never be underestimated. Both ozone depletion and global warming result directly from humanity's relentless, wanton consumption of energy. The methods of this pursuit of energy—the burning of fossil fuels, induction of greenhouse gases into the atmosphere, pollution of the air with other gases, and so on—are changing the atmosphere of the planet at an unprecedented rate. The ultimate environmental impacts, which would affect the entire globe, can only be compared to the aftermath of a nuclear war.

© Patrick Walmsley/Envision

Earth's waters are essential to our survival as a species, and they provide unparalleled beauty as well—yet we continue to risk our future by polluting them.

OZONE DEPLETION AND THE OCEAN

The interdependency and connectedness of our planetary ecosystems can be illustrated if we look at but two segments of the environment: The ozone layer and the ocean. For it is within a few hundred feet of the ocean's surface that the food chain begins, where the small, sometimes microscopic plankton (sea plants) live. (Humans represent the top of the food chain; we are the ultimate consumers of other forms of life on the planet.)

The formidable problems we have created by damaging our ozone layer shrink before the injury that UV radiation can wreak on plankton—and subsequently, on the rest of the food chain.

Plankton, the most abundant community in the sea, are a key element in the food balance that the sea maintains. They form the basis of the food chain—the transfer of energy from one organism to another when the lower organism is eaten. Phytoplankton, through photosynthesis, convert solar energy into food for zooplankton. Zooplankton, in turn, become food for bigger zooplankton, like krill. Krill become food for fish and larger sea life, all the way up to whales. (In Norwegian, *krill* means "whale food." Blues and humpbacks are the main predators of krill, and can swallow up to one ton [.9 metric ton] of them at a time!)

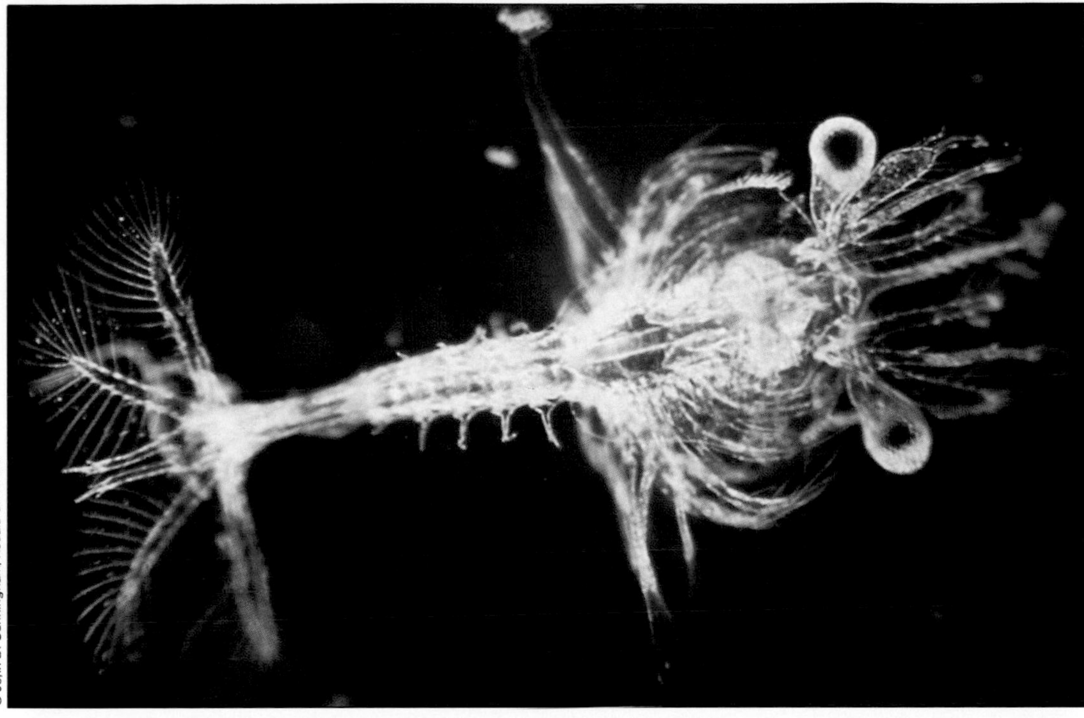

© John D. Cunningham/Visuals Unlimited

© Michael Baytoff

Above, left: ***The zooplankton krill, among the most basic components of the food chain. Found in the ocean, they provide food for fish, whales, and nearly every sea creature in between. Ultraviolet light penetrating the ozone hole can affect populations of krill in a harmful way, jeopardizing all the sea life dependent on them.***

Above: ***A dead fin-back whale washes toward shore outside Deal, New Jersey. While this whale may have expired from natural causes, scientists are finding that toxic chemicals dumped at sea are endangering even the mighty, legendary Moby Dicks.***

Although krill inhabit ocean waters worldwide, dense concentrations of the shrimp-like crustacea exist off the coast of Antarctica. In 1981, the krill population there was deemed to be between 220 million and 6.6 billion. Numerous birds, fish, seals, and whales depend on krill as their primary food source.

Plankton in the Antarctic waters perform another function in addition to their vital role in the food chain. They accomplish 20 percent of all ocean photosynthesis themselves.

But miles and miles above the Southern hemisphere, the ozone layer is thinning. Ultraviolet radiation is falling in greater amounts upon the ocean and the minute plankton that swarm in it. How are they being affected?

Research conducted in Antarctica compared water samples that were exposed to UV light to others that were exposed only to the surrounding, natural light. Phytoplankton were three to five times more productive in the water tank from which UV light was withheld. Water subjected to UV also showed a slower rate of photosynthesis.

UV light can penetrate ocean waters, in calm conditions, to a depth of 60 feet (18 m) or more. Thus, even phytoplankton that live at this lower level may be adversely affected by UV light. Benthic, bottom-dwelling, organisms have also shown a susceptibility to UV radiation.

Because a vast array of other marine life forms ultimately depend on plankton for their continued existence, any substantial change in the numbers or health of these organisms will have far-reaching ecological implications. Should plankton, and eventually krill, be removed from this finely-balanced ecosystem, the entire structure could topple, and the whole marine ecosystem of the Antarctic would be in very serious jeopardy. Ultimately, if the food chain collapses, humanity itself will be at risk.

© James Blank/FPG International

An oil refinery sprawls near Richmond, Virginia. Oil is a finite, non-renewable resource. Offshore oil drilling destroys delicate marine habitats. Land-based operations cause a variety of pollutants to be released into the atmosphere. As overpopulation burdens the planet, we will have to rethink our dependence on petroleum, and learn to harness the energy of the sun instead.

TAKING ACTION

In 1978, in response to the warning that CFC use could destroy the ozone layer, CFC propellants in aerosol sprays were declared illegal in the United States and some other countries. However, CFCs continued to be manufactured for purposes besides the propellant in aerosol cans. Aerosol cans are still the largest source of CFC emissions worldwide, sending 224,000 tons (202,000 metric tons) into the atmosphere annually. Obviously, a solution that targets the global production of CFCs is required if any significant impact is to be felt.

On September 16, 1987, representatives from 24 countries signed a document sponsored by the United Nations Environment Program—the Montreal Protocol on Substances that Deplete the Ozone Layer. The Protocol held that beginning in July 1989, CFC production would be cut to levels produced in 1986. By 1999, CFC production levels would be cut again by half. Halon production, which contributes bromine from fire extinguishers, will be frozen to 1986 levels in 1992. As of January 1990, 53 countries were parties to the Protocol.

The Montreal Protocol is indeed a step in the right direction, but the severity of the ozone problem means that time is of the essence for global endorsement of the treaty. Provisions granted to developing countries that allow for five- and ten-year "grace periods" before CFC production will be limited, but not eliminated, hamper its effectiveness. These countries, in an effort to catch up with the consumption of the rest of the world, are relying more and more on CFCs at a time when it is crucial to ban the chemicals.

The latest evidence on the ever-widening ozone hole has impelled adjustments to the Montreal Protocol that reflect the urgency of the situation. The stringent regulations now endorsed by the treaty delegates demand a total phase-out of CFCs and halons by the year 2000. The adjustments also address the use of carbon tetrachloride, which along with methyl chloroform, accounts for almost 15 percent of all ozone harmful emissions. It is conceivable that if current CFC control measures were employed, all CFC and halon emissions could be slashed by 90 percent. But without stringent adherence to the guidelines of the Montreal Protocol, the goal will not be attained.

Chlorine continues to enter the atmosphere at such a rate that concentrations of the chemical would triple by 2075 even if the majority of the world's countries endorsed the Protocol. Not all of the chlorine and bromine in the atmosphere is due to CFCs, yet the Protocol does not address certain other chemicals that contain these ozone-depleting substances.

With hindsight, we see that a worldwide ban could have been imposed on CFCs shortly after it was discovered that the chemicals were destroying ozone. Even if we do phase out CFCs by the end of this century, their maximum effect will nevertheless be felt 25 years from now. In the most optimistic scenario, the hole in the ozone layer will not be repaired until three-quarters of the next century have passed.

Many environmental organizations feel strongly that the earth cannot wait for a gradual CFC phase-out. They seek a complete elimination of all ozone-depleting chemicals as soon as possible.

Industry in the U.S. has bowed to the urgency of CFC reduction by researching plausible CFC substitutes. Du Pont of Delaware, the leading producer of CFCs in the world, has embarked on a multimillion dollar research effort to develop replacements. Allied Signal of New Jersey, the second-largest CFC producer in the U.S. and one of the foremost CFC manufacturers in the world, began a $250 million program in late 1989 to formulate CFC alternatives.

A company spokesman for Allied Signal said that the chemicals used in place of CFCs will still debilitate the ozone, but will be much less harmful than chlorofluorocarbons. Environmental groups are therefore concerned that these "soft" CFCs being promoted to replace the "hard" CFCs will simply increase the problem of global warming while only partially addressing the ozone depletion issue. Friends of the Earth-Canada, responding to Du Pont's announcement, reminded the public that safer ways to reduce CFC-11 use are immediately available. Its use for refrigeration can be halved in the short term simply by better equipment design, and practicing more responsible maintenance and recycling.

In spite of our knowledge that the ozone layer, essential to the health of the planet and all that lives upon it, is eroding, we continue to unthinkingly destroy our atmosphere. It is difficult to realize that the end result of many of our everyday actions—turning on an air conditioner, pressing an aerosol spray button—can so adversely affect the atmosphere and our own health. Often we rationalize our habits by thinking that they don't make any difference. Yet that belief has contributed to our present crisis.

Unlike a lake clouded with oil slicks or a hillside strewn with litter, we cannot instantly see the effects of ozone depletion. The ozone layer drifts far above us, yet it is essential to our well-being. The fact that it is invisible from our perspective does not mean that it can be ignored. There is only a gossamer strand of ozone to shield us from ourselves.

Top: ***The Arco Oil Refinery in Philadelphia, Pennsylvania. As deep underground reserves are drilled for oil, our overconsumptive lifestyles demand more and more of this precious liquid. What will we do when there is no more oil? How can we decrease our dependency now, saving our injured ozone layer in the process?*** **Bottom:** ***Invisible yet essential to our continued survival as a species, the ozone layer protects us from the sun's radiation.***

The Ocean

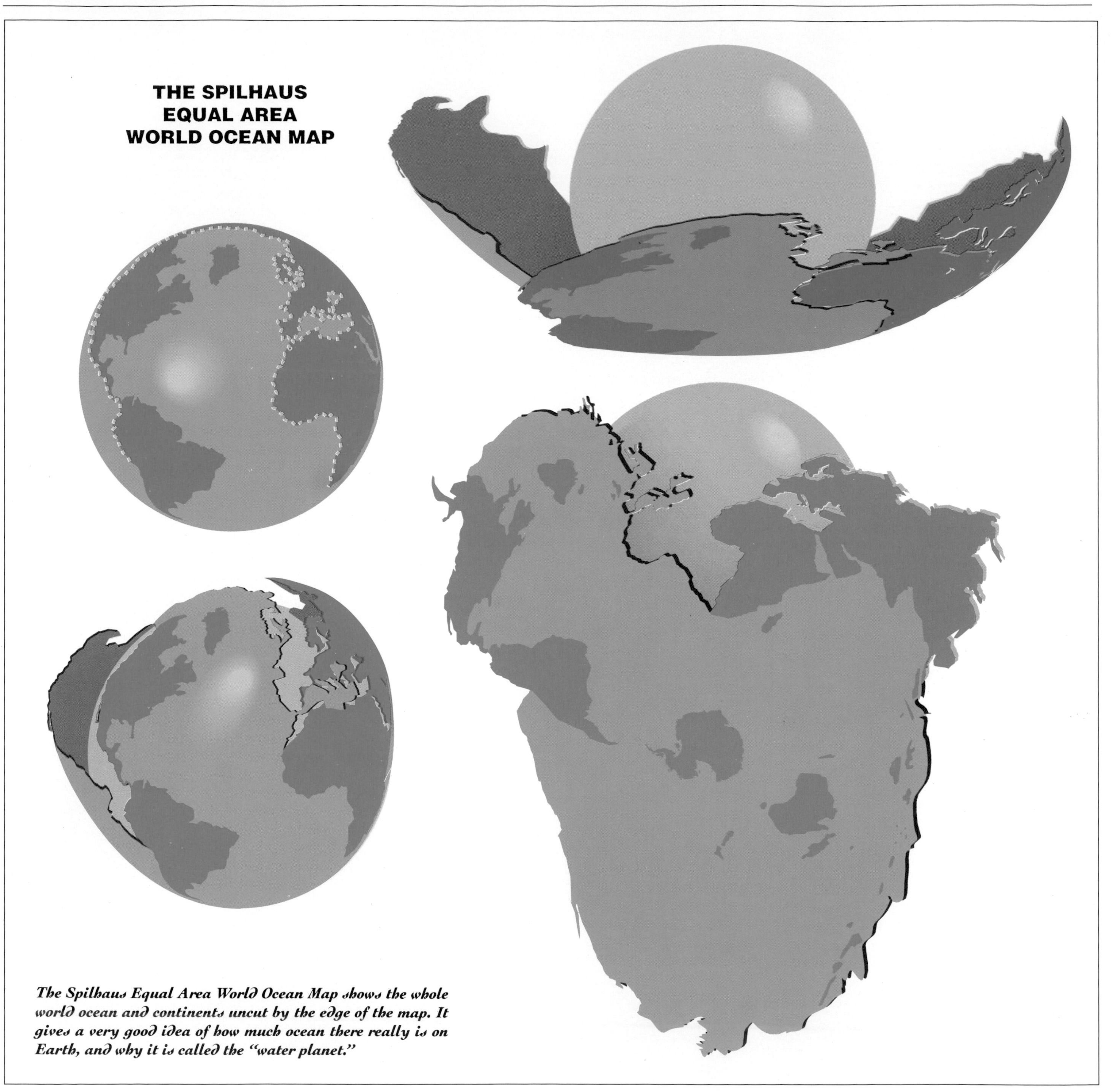

The Spilhaus Equal Area World Ocean Map shows the whole world ocean and continents uncut by the edge of the map. It gives a very good idea of how much ocean there really is on Earth, and why it is called the "water planet."

The utter magnitude of the ocean signifies that we live on a "water planet." For just as the ocean envelops 71 to 73 percent of the earth, our own bodies are 70 percent water. It is water that makes life possible.

If the earth was positioned farther away from the sun, all its water would freeze. If the planet was closer to the sun, the heat would vaporize the water. But the planet's precise location allows the conditions for water, and life, to exist. Solar energy and gravity shift water from the oceans to the atmosphere, where it evaporates. (Water from lakes, rivers, soils, and plants is also carried upward.) The water in the atmosphere falls upon the land and ocean as fresh water. Finally, water on the land is returned to the ocean. This process, known as the hydrological cycle, is repeated continuously to distribute water and sustain life.

The immensity of the ocean can be deceiving. One glance from land's end could lead us to believe that there is a plentiful supply of usable water on the planet. Although 97.1 percent of the world's water is found in the ocean and in saline lakes, it cannot be used for agriculture or drinking. In fact, only 0.003 percent of the total amount of water on earth is considered fresh and usable! Glaciers, ice caps, the atmosphere, and deep soil hold another 2.9 percent of the earth's fresh water, but it is inaccessible. Thus only 0.32 percent remains as fresh water in lakes, rivers, and some underground deposits. Yet 99 percent of these sources are eliminated by pollution, unavailability, and remote locations! Thus the amount from which the world's people must draw is 0.003 percent.

It is also easy to misconstrue the distribution of life within the sea. Nearly all of it is concentrated along the coastal margins, or continental shelves. This zone represents less than 10 percent of the total area of the ocean, yet 90 percent of all marine life dwells there. Ninety-eight percent of the world fish catch occurs within 200 miles (320 km) of land. Tragically, it is in these critical habitats near the shelves, upon which we depend for food and recreation, that most of our polluting has taken place.

The size of the sea has historically been the justification for filling it with every kind of unwanted debris—from explosives and radioactive waste to sewage sludge and ammunition. The reasoning behind ocean dumping is that the ocean is so vast that it can never be saturated to the point where it will cease to function. During the industrialization of America, factories were planned near rivers for a source of power. The coasts became targets for factories, too, because of shipping. The next step was that these waterways became the logical sites for dumping.

Today we know that 85 percent of all ocean pollution begins on the land. Whatever is flushed from the land will make its way, ultimately, to the sea. How can our rivers, streams, and bays be clean if our soils are contaminated with pesticides, chemical lawn applications, and air pollution residues? If our pathways to the ocean are fouled, so is the ocean itself.

Nevertheless, the myth persists that any body of water as huge as the ocean must be able to recover from whatever is poured into it. But the poisonous quality and vast quantity of what we are dumping is beyond the ocean's capacity for self-cleaning.

The debris of a throwaway lifestyle littering the beach at Atlantic City, New Jersey, shows that there is really no such place as "away." Whether we dump at sea, bury our waste in landfills, or burn it, sending tons of pollution into the sky, all of it returns to Earth in some form, to pollute the place where we live. Instead, tin cans and bottles like these should be collected and recycled.

THE MID-ATLANTIC COASTLINE

© Peter Dombrovskis/Envision

Greenpeace examined the decline of one area of the ocean in a report titled, "The Mid-Atlantic Coastline: Ecosystem in Distress," which chronicles the systematic degradation of a section of America's east coast. By looking at this section of the American coastline, perhaps we can begin to understand how others like it become polluted.

The "Mud Dump," located six miles (10 km) off Sandy Hook, New Jersey, was created in 1914 to accept dredge materials from New York harbor. Every year since 1983 enough material to fill three World Trade Center towers has been dumped here. The EPA states such dumping buries benthic organisms, reduces ocean oxygen levels, and elevates concentrations of bacteria and toxic contaminants, such as PCBs. (PCBs, "polychlorinated biphenyls," were once widely used in paints, plastics, and rubber products, as well as electric and heat-transfer equipment.) Known as "persistent" chemicals, PCBs accumulate in the fatty tissues of our bodies. They have been linked to abnormalities in newborns. PCBs are ubiquitous; they have been found in Antarctic penguins, plankton in the Gulf of St. Lawrence, and in mothers' breast milk. The EPA reported that in 1975, nearly one-third of nursing mothers tested showed PCB levels in their milk. The production of PCBs was banned in the U.S. in the late 1970s; they continue to infiltrate the environment from existing sources and as certain industrial by-products. The incineration of garbage creates PCBs in the combustion process, for example.

From 1924 to 1987, municipal sewage sludge came to rest at the "Twelve-Mile Sewage Sludge" Site, about 12 miles (19 km) east of Sea Bright, New Jersey. From 1972 to 1987, 166 billion pounds (75 billion kg) of wet sludge were brought here and dumped in just 80 feet (24 m) of water. According to the EPA, sludge dumping adds more than eight million pounds (4 million kg) of heavy metals—lead, arsenic, mercury, cadmium, and the like—to the marine ecosystem annually. The "Twelve-Mile" site was closed in 1987 due to negative public health and environmental impacts. Local fishermen, referring to its drastic degradation, call that area the "dead sea."

Four hundred thousand cubic yards (304,000 cubic m) of construction debris are dumped every year at the "Cellar Dirt Site," about six miles (10 km) off the coast of New Jersey. The site was opened in 1940.

The "Acid Wastes Dump," located 15 miles (24 km) east of Long Branch, New Jersey, has been in operation since 1948. It is estimated that 118 million pounds (53 million kg) of industrial wastes are unloaded here every year. When infrared satellite photos are taken of this dump, the area glows bright pink, indicating that a wide variety and vast amount of chemicals are being indiscriminately combined and dumped.

From 1960 to 1968, the U.S. military loaded the hulls of old ships with thousands of tons of explosives and chemical munitions, including mustard gas and nerve gas. The vessels were sunk 200 miles (320 km) off the coast of New Jersey and at other points following the coastline. (Between June of 1986 and March of 1987, at least 750 bottlenose dolphins washed ashore along the eastern

seaboard, most outside of New Jersey. They exhibited signs of respiratory trouble and their bodies were pocked with lesions—the same symptoms produced by mustard gas. Robert Schoelkopf, director of the Marine Mammal Stranding Center in Brigantine, New Jersey, attempted to determine a link between the dead dolphins and the insidious cargo sent to the depths two decades earlier. No connection was established, although it has been 13 years since the site of the dumping has been studied for leakage.)

The "Wood-Burning Site," 17 miles (27 km) east of Point Pleasant, New Jersey, was opened in the mid-1960s. Annually, 49,000 tons (44,000 metric tons) of deteriorated waterfront structures are set afire. The wood is covered with creosote, tar, and preservatives. Burning such treated wood generates highly toxic contaminants, like dioxins and furans, that are released into the air. Some escaping pieces, larger than fenceposts, have washed ashore and severely injured bathers.

A manufacturer of clam chowder in Cape May, New Jersey, has been discharging pieces of shell into a ditch that leads to the Atlantic since 1984. The buildup of these shell fragments is responsible for serious oxygen depletion in the water. (New Jersey Public Interest Research Group brought suit against Borden-Snow Foods for overdumping into the ditch. The company agreed to comply with the stipulations of their permit—which still allows them to dump—and they paid a penalty.)

"Site 106," 106 miles (170 km) east of Cape May, is a 100-square mile (260-square km) section of ocean—an area five times the size of Manhattan. In 1988, 16 billion wet tons (14 billion metric tons) of sewage sludge were dumped here. In this sludge was more than 8 million pounds (4 million kg) of heavy metal contaminants and an unknown quantity of toxic organic chemicals. Site 106 lies directly in the path of migrating swordfish, tuna, and other commercially harvested fish. Situated between

© Jeffrey Sylvester/FPG International

Left: ***Waves crash along a rocky Tasmanian seashore, while a sewage pipe (above) empties sludge into the Atlantic near Cape May, New Jersey.***

What has caused so many of these fish to die, all at once? As greater expanses of ocean habitat are exposed to toxic pollutants, scenes like this will occur more frequently. Fish, very sensitive to changes in water temperature, are often killed in large numbers when nuclear power plants release water used in their cooling processes.

the continental shelf and the Gulf Stream waters, the site is subjected to "warm-core eddies" that move in a west-southwesterly direction. From New Jersey, the eddies flow to the Outer Banks of North Carolina before they merge back into the Gulf Stream. This natural action spreads the sludge over an even larger area than the polluted site. Endangered whales, threatened turtles, marlin, and other fish follow the eddies.

The Mid-Atlantic coastline today is returning our treatment of it in kind. Within the last few years, even deep-water fish from areas well past the coast have been afflicted by pollution. Fishermen complain that the fin rot and lesions they used to see in fish near the shore are now appearing in fish much farther out. A shell disease once found only in lobsters taken from polluted harbors is now occurring in lobsters from these same deep off-shore waters.

Clearly, we have gone about our business on land and sea without the guiding influence of a conscience, or a second thought for the future of our world. We have treated the great, life-giving ocean as a garbage can for our most volatile wastes. Unfortunately, conditions along the eastern seaboard are not unique.

The deck of a sludge barge. Dumping adds millions of pounds of heavy metals to the marine ecosystem annually, ensuring unhealthy habitats for creatures below the waves. Fishermen report an increase in diseased catches, linked with the degraded quality of water in certain areas.

SLUDGE DUMPING

The ocean is still the major receptacle for sewage sludge around the world. Although some governments, like those in the Netherlands and Norway, are trying to find solutions to the problem, the situation in Europe varies widely from country to country. Currents off the coast of England bring the sludge back towards Europe, and the Netherlands receive the brunt of the pollution.

In the United States, the passage of the Ocean Dumping Act in 1988 (sludge loadings into the sea must end by December 31, 1991, or an escalating fee will be charged) has not halted the problem. After the 1991 deadline, ocean dumping still will not be prohibited—it will just begin to cost excessively more. Sludge dumpers will simply pay the fines, with taxpayers' money, because they have no firm plans yet to process the sludge on the land.

Environmentalists are calling for the building of plants to process the sludge into compost. The passage of strict laws to prevent chemical companies from flushing their wastes through their sewer systems must occur first. If pre-treatment laws were rigidly enforced, a clean, compostable sewage sludge would result.

INDUSTRIAL WASTE WATER

The fate of industrial waste water is of particular concern. In the United States alone, the total industrial waste water output is over 6.4 trillion gallons (23 trillion l) a year! Three-fourths of this amount is discharged directly into nearby sources of water; the remainder is sent through a treatment plant first, although this process does not guarantee the removal of dangerous compounds. Industries are the primary contributors of heavy metals and toxic organic chemicals in publicly-owned waste water treatment facilities (POWTs). According to the EPA, industry delivers 80 percent of all heavy metal loadings and 92 percent of priority organic pollutants, yet it represents only 12 percent of the total flow, with households and businesses generating the rest.

POWTs are designed essentially to deal with pathogens (disease-producing organisms), solids, and odors. Somewhat more advanced systems can remove a portion of the nutrients present in sludge. However, no POWTs are equipped to deal with the heavy metals that are commonly discharged into municipal sewers, nor can any of them destroy the toxic organic chemicals that end up in municipal waste water systems. These dangerous metals and toxics, along with the treated waste water, are discharged into waterways, deposited in the sludge, or, as with the more volatile chemicals, released into the air.

A case in point is the Ciba-Geigy pharmaceutical manufacturing company of Tom's River, New Jersey. Since 1966, the company has operated an outfall pipe that extends a half mile (.8 km) into the ocean. (In June of 1989, Governor Thomas Kean signed Bill S-128 into law, which ended direct ocean discharge of private industrial waste. But Ciba-Geigy were allowed to use their pipe for another year before the law took effect.)

The company claims that about 2 million gallons (8 million l) of chemically-tainted waste water passed through the plant's on-site treatment plant daily, before going through the pipe to the ocean. But Save Our Ocean, an environmental group instrumental in "plugging" the pipe, has records that show the actual amount released was actually more than three million gallons (13 million l) per day, and at times reached a high of seven million gallons (27 million l) in a 24-hour period.

A recent laboratory study submitted to New Jersey's Department of Environmental Protection found that sand and surf in the vicinity of the pipeline contained cadmium, mercury, nickel, chromium, benzene, chloronated hydrocarbons, and PAHs, one of the most carcinogenic of all chemical substances. Although Ciba has attempted to convince the public that their outgoing effluent is sufficiently treated to be safe, another recent study showed that the treated water was still so impure that 30 million mutagenic doses of chemicals were being piped into the ocean every day.

Tom's River is known as a "cancer-cluster" community. Its population is plagued with 50 to 90 percent more of certain cancers than the average population. A high incidence of childhood cancer is also documented in the vicinity. One of the nation's worst Superfund sites (areas requiring federal environmental cleanup) is on the grounds of Ciba-Geigy, where at least 100,000 drums of toxic waste are buried. The drums are leaking and contaminating wells on adjacent properties.

Far left: ***Chemical effluent being pumped into a river by a nearby factory. Rivers used as dumpsites are a significant cause of ocean pollution, as all of them empty into the sea. By keeping these corridors clean, we can improve the health of the ocean.*** **Above:** ***Another example of sending unwanted materials "away." Whether this effluent flows to the sea or percolates underground, eventually we will be the recipients of its effects.***

© Jack Casement/Envision

The North Sea is presently the only place where toxic waste is burned at sea.

THE NORTH SEA

The North Sea is another ocean "hot spot" that is being bombarded with pollution. World Watch Institute reports that 11,000 tons (9,900 metric tons) of heavy metals and five million tons (4.5 million metric tons) of sewage are released into this part of the ocean every year. Greenpeace has publicized the fact that the countries bordering the North Sea have witnessed wide-scale deaths of marine mammals, algal blooms, and countless hauls of diseased fish.

Yet this highly vulnerable area is under attack again—this time, from a technology that has already been instrumental in poisoning the land: incineration.

The incinerator ships that ply the North Sea burn liquid toxic waste. The idea was first embraced by West Germany in 1969, as a method of avoiding the dumping of toxic wastes directly into the ocean.

The London Dumping Convention, formed in 1972, regulates international toxic waste disposal on the high seas. They described ocean incineration as "an interim method. . . pending the development of environmentally better solutions." In this case, interim has been in progress for almost 20 years.

At the North Seas Ministries Conference in 1988, a resolution was passed that incineration on ships in the North Sea must stop by 1995. Currently, toxic waste is not burned at sea in any other location.

However, with gross revenues of $2 billion last year, the ocean incineration industry is not expected to just disappear. Greenpeace has tracked industry representatives in Canada, Ireland, the South Pacific, and the Caribbean. Countries in more southern waters, frantically trying to attain the same economic pinnacle as their northern neighbors, have toxic wastes that need to be disposed of, too.

The most logical argument against ocean incineration is the possibility of an accident. Ponder this equation: a tanker-size load of poisonous liquid plus rough weather plus a crew striving to function under a cloud of toxic fumes. Then imagine the effects of such a cargo inadvertently poured into the sea. An accident of this magnitude would be catastrophic for the marine ecosystem, and is all too possible.

Yet in weighing the "advantages" and "disadvantages" of burning at sea, the U.S. government in 1986 considered igniting 700,000 gallons (2,660,000 l) of PCB-laced oil in the North Atlantic. First, however, the oil had to be moved to a location from which it could be picked up by a boat. That would have entailed a distance of 1,480 miles (2,368 km)—from Emelle, Alabama, location of the world's largest toxic waste landfill, to Philadelphia, Pennsylvania.

The track record for conveying toxic materials by land is poor. The Department of Transportation states that 12 incidents that involve deaths, serious injury and/or damage over $50,000 occur daily in the U.S. One million pounds (450,000 kg) of pollutants leaked into American waterways in 1984 because of land-based accidents, according to the U.S. Coast Guard.

Fish gasp for air in polluted water. Chemical companies discharging waste into nearby streams endanger the plants and animals living there. Detergents with phosphates stimulate plant growth in streams and lakes, cutting off oxygen and killing fish. Read the labels of the products you buy.

Referring to the accident potential from the proposed North Atlantic test burn in 1986, a government environmental impact statement admitted that a spill could mean "a serious public health hazard. . . cleanup would be difficult and expensive, if possible at all. Effects of contamination could be widespread and possibly long-lasting."

Like garbage incinerators, oceangoing furnaces create more pollution than they remedy. Besides the fact that not all of the material sent to the burners is destroyed, new toxic substances are formed in the process. Scientists know that dioxins, furans, and other highly toxic compounds are in these new substances, but no one knows for sure exactly what the properties of these poisonous new chemicals are. Yet tons of hazardous liquid waste are being burned regardless of the consequences.

A new approach to waste is being taken by environmentalists such as Dr. Paul Connett of Work on Waste U.S.A. who believe that what most people call "garbage" is really unrecovered resources being thrown away. . . only to be re-created at tremendous costs of time, energy, and money. Instead of spending billions of dollars trying to perfect the destruction of our discarded materials through incineration, we should be putting our efforts into recovering them. The landfill crisis is a timely reminder at the local level that you cannot run a throwaway society on a finite planet. . . but other major dangers such as the greenhouse effect and the damage to the ozone layer have shown us that human activities threaten our world. We cannot conduct business as usual. Thus, from both the local planning point of view, and from a planetary perspective, we need to search for ways to move from waste management to resource management.

This approach can be applied to toxic substances and their legacy of harm to the environment. An example is the heavy metals contained in batteries. Over 70 percent of communities in Japan have programs to prevent dumping of batteries. The batteries are removed, then collected and stored in warehouses; in addition, Clean Japan Center is pursuing a pilot project to recycle some of the metals in the batteries. Many of the metals, in addition to being toxic, are also in short supply, so the program makes both environmental and economic sense. The message to battery companies is simple: If you can't recycle the toxic metals from the batteries, then do not make them. Either recycle or find non-toxic substitutes.

There are successful on-site waste reduction and re-use programs being practiced today. In Bonn, West Germany, industries are streamlining recycling methods to remove the ingredients in toxic waste that can be used again. New land-based technologies take advantage of the heat value generated by waste—they harness it to make operations more efficient. These and other strategies being developed show a conscious effort to change a habit of abuse. The next step should be to phase out production of toxics altogether, and replace them with benign substances.

© Daniel W. Gotshall/Visuals Unlimited

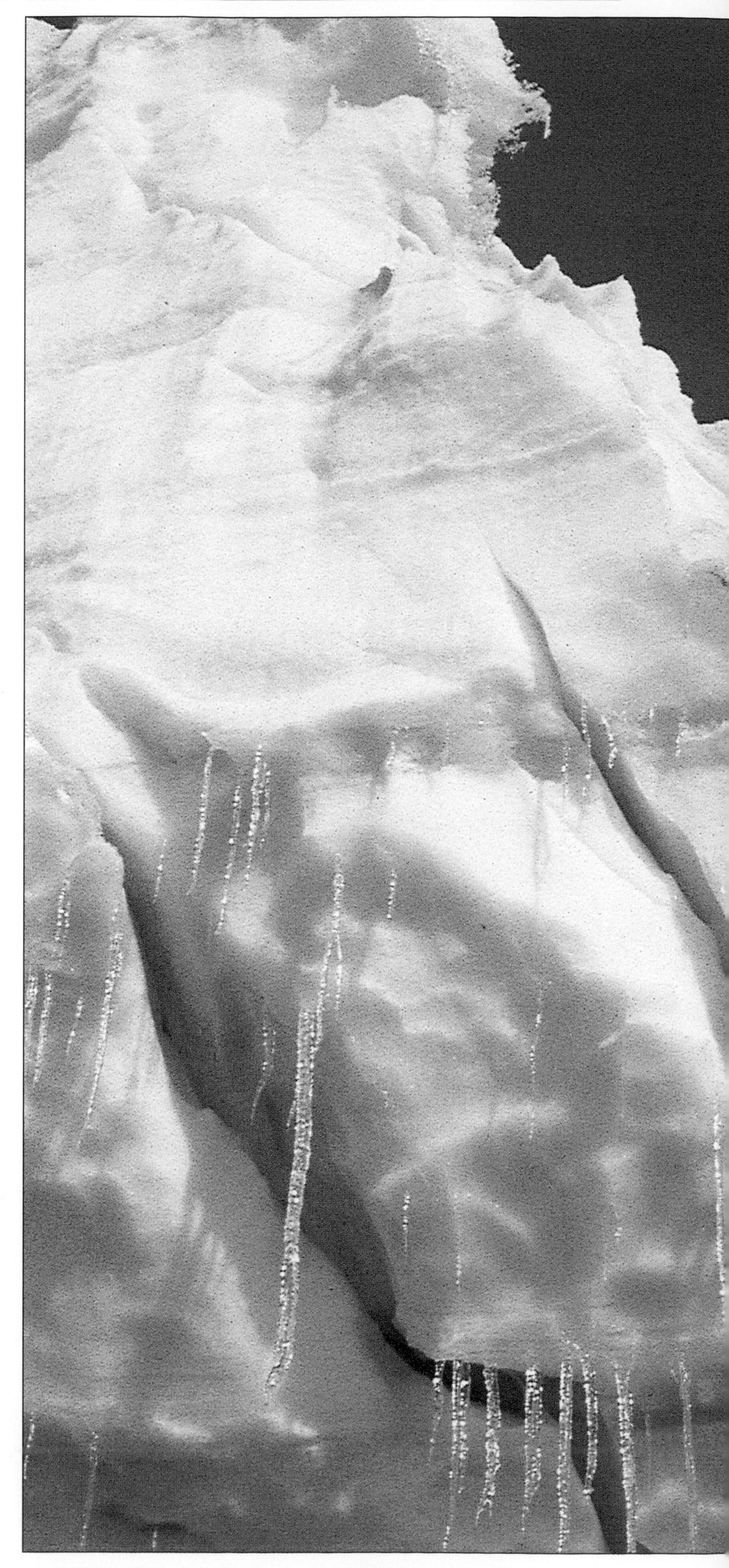

© Frank T. Awbrey/Visuals Unlimited

THE GREENHOUSE EFFECT AND THE OCEAN

A ban on ocean incineration for the sake of our beleaguered atmosphere must prevail. The possibility of producing more greenhouse gases and the further weakening of the ozone layer should serve as a warning not to proceed with the burning of toxic wastes on land or sea.

One of the functions the ocean performs is to store and distribute energy from the sun. It has been called a "global heat exchanger." Climatic changes would be much more rapid without the stabilizing effect of the ocean.

A factor known as the "thermal delay" needs to be considered when we discuss the greenhouse effect in relation to the ocean. There is a delay of at least 10 to 50 years between the time the greenhouse gases are added to the atmosphere and the time that the full effect of their warming can be gauged. The delay is due to the fact that it takes a much longer amount of time to warm the oceans than it does to warm the atmosphere. The greater the greenhouse gas warming, the longer the ocean thermal delay. For example, if a doubled amount of carbon dioxide in the atmosphere resulted in a 7°F (4°C) warming, the delay before we would feel the full effect of that warming would be 50 to 100 years. Conversely, if the same amount of carbon dioxide resulted in a 2°F (1.5°C) warming, the delay before we would feel its full effect might be just 15 years.

During the past century, there has been a 1.7°F (0.4°C) warming of the ocean. On the average, sea level has risen accordingly four to six inches (10 to 15 cm). A continued warming will accelerate the rise of sea level. Scientists project a 12-inch (30-cm) rise, with as much as half an inch (1.5 cm) by the middle of the next century. The effects of such a rise would be wide-ranging. Tropical cyclones may appear more frequently and strike with greater force than we have known. Islands and coastal areas would be subject to flooding. Some may be inundated completely. Saltwater intrusion would reduce water supplies on the coasts. The possibility of a three- to six-foot (1- to 2-m) sea level rise by 2100 could eliminate 50 to 80 percent of the American coastal wetlands. Beaches would be eroded by 66 to 200 feet (20 to 60 m) or more if a 12-inch (30-cm) rise takes place. The melting of the Greenland and alpine glaciers could each contribute 4 to 12 inches (10 to 30 cm) more to sea level rise through 2100.

Left: ***A soda can rests beneath the sea, an alien object in a watery world. Some companies are endorsing the creation of artificial reefs using hazardous waste and garbage to replace natural reefs that have been destroyed by chemical dumping and other forms of underwater exploitation. Who would invade the caverns of the sea with poison?*** **Right:** ***A glacier looms at Cape Bird, Ross Island, Antarctica. Global warming contributes to the melting of glaciers, which will eventually augment a rise in sea level.***

The residue of humanity collects on the ocean floor, while a lifeform grows within a garden of trash. Through this maze of pollution swim fish and other ocean creatures, searching for food to keep themselves alive and healthy.

LOSS OF HABITAT

Because the ocean appears to be a limitless resource, our relationship to it has been one of exploitation. The most disturbing result of ocean dumping is the widespread chronic degradation and loss of habitat. Pollution is killing our coral reefs and other unique ecosystems that are the most vital links in the food chain. By assailing these unique ecosystems, we are debasing the food chain. We are tampering with the sea's ability to produce adequate levels of fish that we depend upon for protein.

As an example, consider the ocean in the vicinity of the Philippine Islands, where 95 percent of the coral reefs have been destroyed by cyanide fishing.

Cyanide fishing began a decade ago when a corporation in Manila found a simple, lucrative way to supply tropical fish to pet shops in the United States and Europe. The company hired fishermen to pump industrial sodium cyanide into offshore coral reefs. The fish living in the reefs, stunned by the cyanide, would be forced to the surface and were easily scooped into nets.

The fish died prematurely several months later, but by that time, they had been sold in pet stores. Customers, unaware of what caused the fish to die, would return to the store to buy more.

Cyanide fishing is illegal in the Philippines, but environmental laws there are not enforced. (Incidents of fishermen with machine guns on their boats as well as nets have been reported.) The owner of the company in Manila admitted that in order for him to operate, the chemical had to be smuggled in and officials had to be bribed.

The International Marinelife Alliance, with a chapter in the Philippines, has been showing fishing companies alternative ways of capturing fish. Now divers chase the fish into nets.

The company guilty of destroying the reefs has supposedly rejected cyanide, and is trying to teach other companies to do the same. But given the near-obliteration of the reefs, and the long-term effects of cyanide-polluted water, how much did it really cost to buy a pretty fish?

The bounty of the sea is being defiled in a different way in the North Pacific, where 30,000 to 40,000 miles (48,000 to 64,000 km) of ocean are being biologically "strip-mined."

In this fairly empty stretch of ocean north of Hawaii, south of the Aleutians, east of Japan, and west of California, Asian drift-net boats have been busy since the early 1980s. Working from 4 to 10 months out of the year, a fleet of boats, 750 to 1,000 strong, each set a driftnet loose at dusk to capture squid. Each net is 30 miles (48 km) long and forms a wall beneath the waves 30 feet (9 m) deep. In the morning, radar is employed to retrieve the nets. What is in them? Besides squid, every fish, fur seal, dolphin, and porpoise that swam in the upper water column all night long.

The trawler crews keep the fish and discard the other bodies heaped in the netting. Because many of these nets are lost or abandoned, they continue to drift aimlessly through the sea. As they do not disintegrate, they keep trapping unsuspecting fish and marine mammals. The netted animals, unable to escape, become bait for other sea life, such as birds, that are soon just as hopelessly enmeshed. Tens of thousands of porpoises and dolphins are killed in the driftnets annually. It is estimated that 35,000 to 50,000 fur seals die each year of entanglement in the monofilament nets.

© S. Ross/Visuals Unlimited

© Michael Baytoff

Left: ***A fishing catch. Ruthless harvests using deadly driftnets capture not only fish and squid, but birds, seals, dolphins, and porpoises.*** **Above:** ***This Atlantic bottle-nosed dolphin suffocated from the plastic net coiled around its mouth. Nets loosed in the ocean, as well as plastic debris carried from the land, bring many noble sea creatures to untimely ends.***

The countries engaged in this abominable practice are Japan, South Korea, and Taiwan. The area in which they operate is one of the most fertile fishing grounds in the ocean—a cold, nutrient-rich expanse that is filled with varieties of fish. Salmon and steelhead trout that migrate from Oregon, Washington, and British Columbia head for the North Pacific. In 1988, Alaskan fishermen expected a catch of 40 million pink salmon. What they actually took was 12 million; the missing salmon were probably immature specimens that had been snared in the driftnets before they could return to North American streams to spawn.

The drift-net fleets know that it is illegal to catch or keep young salmon or trout. However, these fish are considered a delicacy in Europe, and the slaughter continues. Undersized salmon were delivered in staggering amounts to the wholesale markets in Taiwan and Singapore in 1988, where they were processed before being sold.

Biologists are gravely concerned that removing so much of the food chain will have drastic repercussions on the North Pacific ecosystem. If the catch is large and sustained year after year, the balance of the food chain will be changed, because a significant part of it has been taken away. There is no way of knowing the outcome of that change.

The three countries participating in driftnetting in the North Pacific are not fettered by laws or regulations. They have also refused to restrict or acknowledge the scope of what they do. Spokespersons from each country have declared that unintended nettings of marine life are "minimal." When environmentalists proposed to put satellite tracking devices on the Japanese boats, however, Japan would not allow it.

Environmentalists have been lobbying for a ban on driftnetting. A recent agreement among the U.S., Canada, and Japan allowed observers to monitor four percent of Japan's drift-net fleet for a two-to-four-month period. Some members of Congress feel that the agreement is an important first step for the collection of hard data on the extent of damage to the ecosystem. Others insist that it does nothing to phase out driftnetting, and offers no protection for marine life. Meanwhile, the Taiwanese and South Korean fleets still comb the sea completely unmonitored.

In the North Pacific, what is being withdrawn from the ocean could have as detrimental an effect as what pollution is adding elsewhere.

A Kemp's Ridley sea turtle enmeshed in a net. This is the legacy of technology without responsibility.

A loggerhead sea turtle surfaces to snap at floating plastic, which resembles a jellyfish. Ingested plastic causes death in birds, turtles, and other ocean life. Plastic is glutting the planet. Even the manufacturing of plastic is dangerous, creating some of the most toxic compounds known.

THE PLASTIC TRAP

Driftnets are not the only forms of plastic in the ocean. Often, what we produce and throw away on the land arrives at the threshold of the sea. In the United States in 1987, 15.2 billion pounds (7 billion kg) of plastic was produced, and sold in the form of lids, bottles, bags, and other items. Littering, sewage outfall, plastic processing activities, and transportation of solid waste by barges all lead to an increase of plastics in the ocean.

A recent 150-mile (240-km) survey of North Carolina beaches tallied 8000 plastic bags in a three-hour walk. Offshore, a turtle was found with 15 bags in its stomach; a whale had swallowed 50.

It is easy for marine life to mistake plastic debris for food. Turtles and mammals eat sections of plastic sheeting that resemble jellyfish. A turtle located in the New York area had ingested 590 feet (177 m) of heavy-duty fishing line.

After being synthesized from petrochemicals, plastic emerges in a raw state known as "pellets." These pellets have even fooled researchers in laboratories, who confused them with fish eggs. A study of Alaskan seabirds showed that 70 percent of the plastic they pecked from the water was in the form of pellets. Scientists theorize that seabirds selectively choose the pellets over other debris because they look so much like fish eggs, fish and squid eyes, and planktonic organisms. The plastic that seabirds ingest floats at the same level as the food they would normally eat, and even matches the color of their food—white, yellow, tan, and brown pellets are the ones most frequently chosen.

A sea animal does not have to eat plastic to be harmed by it. Seals are the major victims of six-pack rings that act as collars, constricting their throats as they grow. Eventually, strangulation causes death. Fish, birds, and sea lions also become entangled in these rings. A three-hour walk along the Texas coastline recently resulted in the collection of 15,600 six-pack rings.

In 1975, the National Academy of Sciences estimated that oceangoing vessels dumped 14 billion pounds (6 billion kg) of garbage overboard per year. More than 10 million pounds (4 billion kg) of that garbage was believed to be plastic. But Annex V of the International Convention for the Prevention of Pollution from Ships (nicknamed "MARPOL" Protocol, signifying "MARine POLlution"), adopted in 1987, prohibited all dumping of plastic wastes from all ships at sea. Vessels are required to dispose of their refuse dockside. However, public vessels, including Navy ships, do not have to come into compliance with Annex V until 1994. And, furthermore, Annex V is an optional part of MARPOL. Although 39 countries to date have ratified MARPOL, not all of them have signed Annex V. For oceangoing vessels, disposing of garbage at sea is simply considered the easiest and least expensive way to deal with the problem.

When will the scourge of plastic in the ocean be relieved? Not until we learn how to deal with the problem on the land. Although several kinds of plastic are degradable, others are not. It is becoming increasingly obvious that even though we may have the technology to produce something, ethically, we are not bound to actually produce it, if harm to the environment results.

Left: ***A Hawksbill sea turtle hatchling entangled in monofilament fishline. This little, doomed turtle will never experience the joys of its wondrous habitat. Thoughtlessly discarded and escaped nets will claim many more lives.*** **Above:** ***Among the litter on a beach lies a dead gull, a victim of monofilament fishline. Consumers can help by boycotting plastic, and using wax paper or cellulose bagging instead.***

THE EXXON VALDEZ OIL SPILL

A brutal reminder that our greed has exceeded the limits of common sense occurred on March 24, 1989, when the Exxon oil tanker *Valdez* rammed into a reef in Prince William Sound, Alaska. More than 12½ million gallons (48 million l) of crude oil invaded the ocean. No one can predict the full impact of this event.

The *Valdez* and ships like it routinely transport huge quantities of oil, though we lack the capability of cleaning up even 10 percent of it in case of a major spill. Is our need for oil, a non-renewable resource, so great that such a risk is justified?

A patch of oil the size of a quarter will kill a bird or an otter. Oil coating the bodies of birds and marine animals smothers them. The body-insulation of warm-blooded animals is disrupted before death. Volatile gases settle in the livers and kidneys of victims that may live a little longer, continually poisoning them. More than 20 tons of animals, including 600 sea otters and 9,400 birds, were less than the total death count, which mounts as more animals succumb.

Every time *any* oil tanker parts the waves with its bow, the risk of a spill is being taken again. It is often argued that environmentalists' proposals for improving prevention, containment, and clean-up of oil spills—as well as spill liability, compensation and tanker safety—are too expensive or cannot survive rigorous cost/benefit analyses. According to Clifton Curtis of The Oceanic Society, however, these programs could add only a few cents to the consumer price of a barrel of oil in a nation whose energy problems can most readily be solved by energy efficiency, lower consumption of oil from Alaska and other areas, and alternative sources of energy. These are programs designed to protect our marine environment, and they offer enormous benefits to America and all societies—benefits so valuable that they are beyond financial calculation. Their minimal costs must be measured against the immense long-term costs of environmental damage.

Perhaps the tragedy of the Exxon *Valdez* was felt so keenly because of the part of the world in which it happened. The Environmental Policy Institute describes Prince William Sound this way: "It is filled with pristine chains of islands and its coastal areas are flush with fish and delicate rookeries of vital bird species. Its waters are fundamental migratory paths and playgrounds for whales, seals and otters alike." The spill happened on the precipice of the month of April, normally the most important days for reproduction of herring species and seaward migration of juvenile salmon in Alaskan waters. Salmon hatcheries are likewise in jeopardy; the salmon run in Prince William Sound is one of the world's largest.

Lest we forget the magnitude of the spill too soon, the inordinately frigid waters of the Sound will remind us. They will cause the toxicity of the oil to linger years longer than it would have in more temperate seas.

In the undulating depths of the sea are the mysteries of life. . . creatures that inhabit the realm of the ocean floor. . . whales that sing to each other as they part the waves. . . dolphins that cavort with sheer joy. Through the lacy fronds of sea plants and in coral caverns, the deepest parts of our

© Gary Braasch

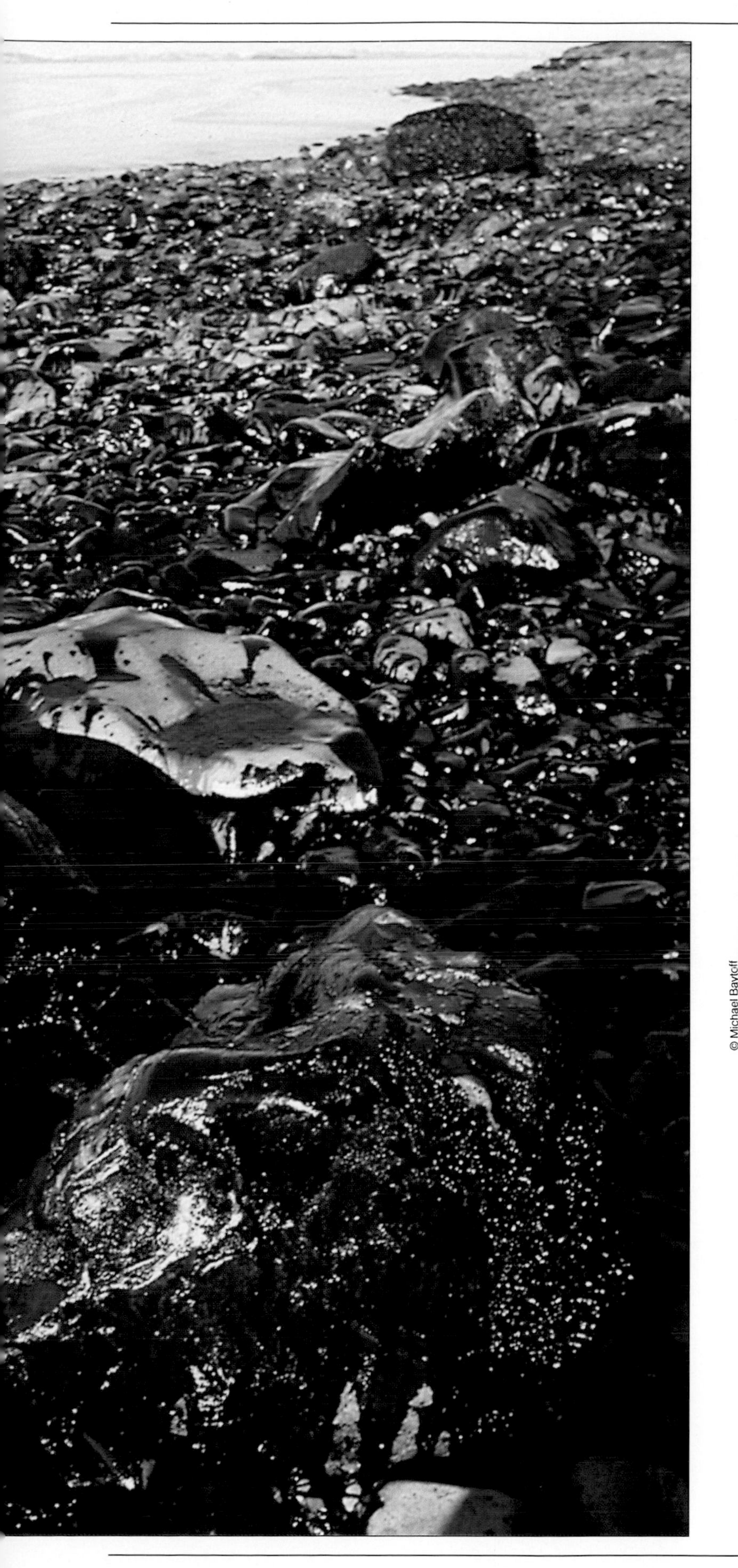

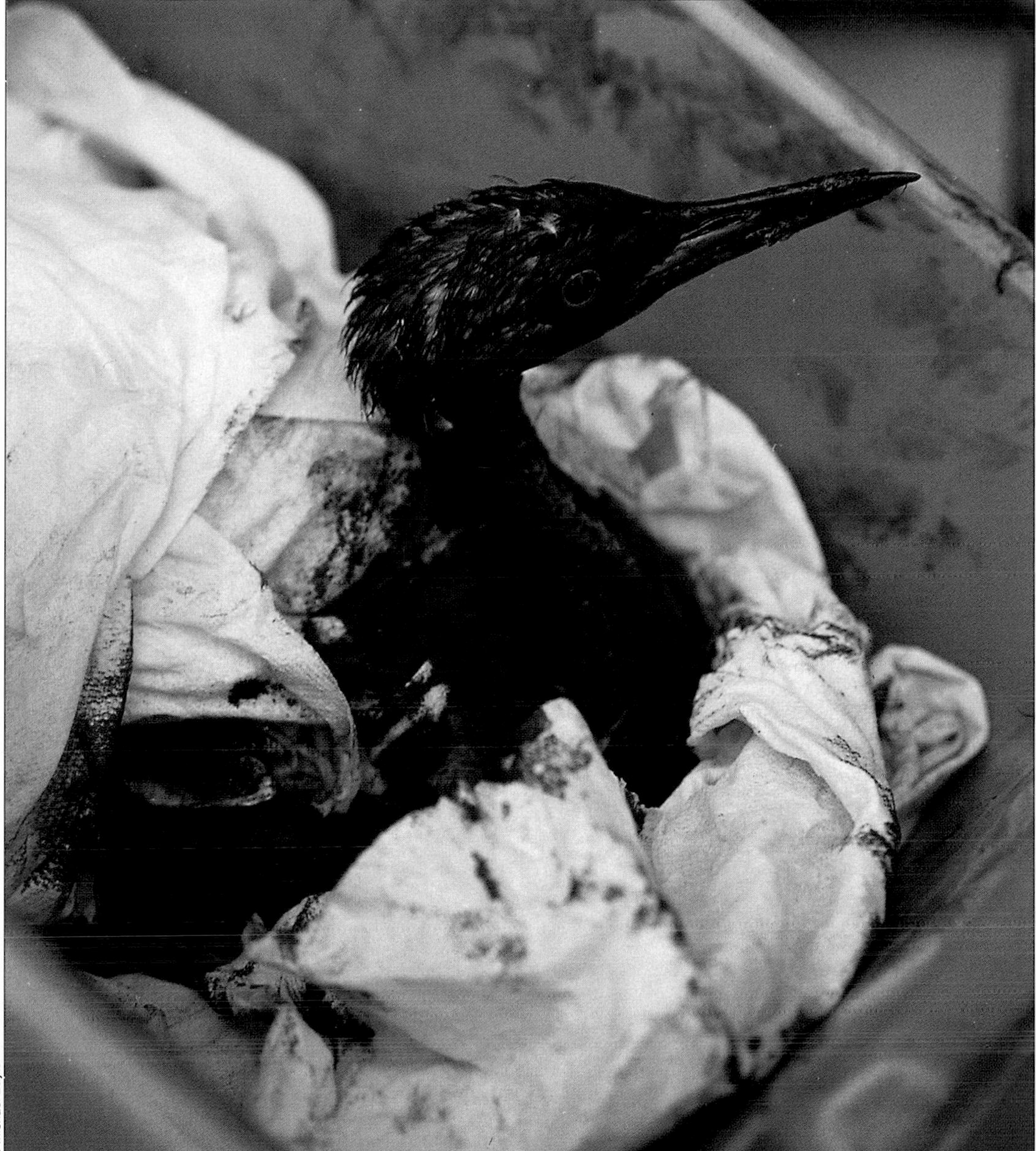

© Michael Baytoff

imaginations remember our salty origins. For centuries, people have marveled at what swam beneath the white-capped crests. Mermaids, sirens, even Triton on his watery throne have beckoned us to expand the horizons of our minds to match the grandeur of the boundless ocean.

It is time to gaze anew at the sea, at the seashells clogged with garbage at our feet, and envision the magic and power of the water that gives us life. As beings on a water planet, if we continue to imperil the ocean, we continue to imperil ourselves.

Left: ***An Alaskan shoreline slathered with oil, the first night after the*** **Exxon Valdez** ***oil spill.***
Above: ***An oil-smeared grebe, rescued, awaits cleaning. It is immaterial to this bird who owned the tanker responsible for the spill in Prince William Sound. Tankers haul oil across dangerous distances to heat all of our homes.***

THE GREAT LAKES

© Wayne Lankinen/Valan Photos

The shores of majestic Lake Superior on a winter's day. Superior is not only the largest of the Great Lakes, but also the largest body of fresh water in the world.

From the air, these giant bodies of water resemble a jagged oasis of turquoise. The smallest of the Lakes, Erie, measures 50 miles (80 km) wide. The largest, Lake Superior, could hold all the water in Lakes Huron, Michigan, Erie, and Ontario, plus three more Lake Eries! With a coastline 150 miles (240 km) long and a surface 350 miles (560 km) wide, Superior also holds the distinction of being one of the world's largest lakes.

Together, the five Great Lakes cover almost 95,000 square miles (247,000 square km). They are embraced by two countries (the United States and Canada) and touch eight states (New York, Pennsylvania, Ohio, Michigan, Indiana, Illinois, Wisconsin, and Minnesota) and one province (Ontario). A series of 80,000 inland lakes within their ecosystem have a combined area greater than that of Lake Erie. Another 2,342 miles (3,747 km) of connecting waterways make the Great Lakes the most extensive inland water transportation network on earth. The Great Lakes "basin"—the lakes and all the soils that drain into them—form America's heartland. An incredible diversity of wildlife inhabits the basin's marshes, bays, forests, and shores.

One of the last surviving packs of wolves roams the ridges and valleys of Isle Royale in Lake Superior, Michigan. Their chief prey is the moose.

Some populations of otters and mink colonize along the lake shores of the basin, although more are found near inland bodies of water. Deer and racoons amble through the woodlands.

Eagles and osprey, once endangered, can be spotted soaring majestically, scanning the landscape for prey. Other fish-eating birds like herring gulls, terns, and several varieties of cormorants are frequently seen. The spindly legs of herons resemble the reed-like stems of cattails that ring the lagoons. A stab of their long sharp beaks nets a meal of frogs, fish, small crabs, water snakes, or large grasshoppers. Loons, mergansers, and ducks paddle through ponds. On the sandy dunes of the lakes, little piping plovers nest in the pebbles.

Many types of fish inhabit the waters of the basin. Coho and Chinook salmon have been successfully introduced into Lake Michigan. Although lake trout are native, the rainbow and brown are also at home here. Yellow perch, smelt, and walleye thrive.

The beauty of the Great Lakes makes them one of the most visited areas of the country. Photographers and hikers are rewarded by scenic views nearly everywhere they look. Tall fir forests scent the air with pine. The windswept waters of Superior crash in plumes of white foam against craggy rocks. Gulls perch on eroded cliffs. The sandy beaches of Lake Michigan are lapped by retreating waves. Like outstretched fingers of gold, rays of the sinking sun burnish deep-blue skies.

Twenty percent of all the fresh water on the planet, and almost all of the fresh water available in the United States, comes from the Great Lakes. Forty million people—32 percent of Canadians and 13 percent of Americans—live in the basin. Over half of this population depends on the Great Lakes system for their drinking water. For every basin resident, food, transportation, recreation, electric power, tourism, and employment are inextricably linked with the lakes, along with one other factor: health.

In a 1985 report, scientists claimed that people who live in the Great Lakes basin accumulate significantly more toxins in their bodies, and may be in a greater-risk category for illnesses, than people living virtually anywhere else in North America. Why?

Along the harbors and coasts of this extraordinary aquatic resource reside one-fifth of the manufacturers in the United States; half of Canada's manufacturers are centered in the same corridor. The shores of Lakes Superior, Michigan, and Huron are studded with wood processing plants. In the channel between Lakes Huron and Erie are crowded oil refineries, auto factories, and chemical corporations. The Niagara River between Lakes Erie and Ontario is lined with chemical, steel, and plastics factories. Mills and mines crisscross the entire basin. The industrial "pocket" of the Great Lakes also produces or uses 30,000 chemicals, and generates 32 percent of all American, and 41 percent of all Canadian, hazardous wastes.

The wildlife of the Great Lakes region once thrived in a pristine environment; today it is rare to find wildlife unaffected by pollution.

© Ron W. Bohr

WILDLIFE OF THE LAKES

The health of wildlife in a given habitat is considered a reflection of the habitat itself. What are the birds and animals of the Great Lakes telling us?

The Canadian Institute for Environmental Law and Policy reports that numerous species living near the shores of the Great Lakes are entirely unable to reproduce. These species include bald eagles, osprey, and mink. Birds that eat Great Lakes fish, like cormorants and gulls, are giving birth to babies that have serious physical deformities. In Green Bay, Wisconsin, and Saginaw Bay, Michigan, fish-eating birds are regularly born with crossed bills, which condemns them to starvation, and club feet. According to Greenpeace, half of the birds in Saginaw Bay on Lake Huron are now showing defects.

In January 1989, a study in Bay City, Michigan, showed a high rate of birth defects in fish-eating birds in the basin. In the unhatched eggs of a growing number of birds, particularly caspian terns and cormorants, yolk sacs were found hanging on the outside of the embryo. Such a deformity is a common symptom of PCB poisoning. Rates of birth defects of caspian terns on Lakes Michigan and Huron are more than 30 times higher than they were in the 1960s. In 1987, in some tern colonies with 400 or more eggs, only a quarter of the eggs hatched; the chicks lived but 12 days. So far, nine species of birds, including the Great Blue Heron, have been born with crossed beaks.

© Chris Huss/The Wildlife Collection

The bald eagle (**Haliaeetus leucocephalus*****) once ranged throughout North America. Today this noble bird's survival is threatened by habitat destruction, pollution, and illegal hunting.* Above: *A school of chinook salmon.***

In the St. Lawrence River, at the eastern end of the Great Lakes, a population of beluga whales has declined so severely that it faces extinction. This population is the most southern concentration of belugas in the world, and is considered geographically isolated from northern belugas. The St. Lawrence whales, several thousand strong prior to 1949, were counted at 1,500 in the 1960s and then dropped to about 350 in 1978. The whales have been protected by law from hunting, killing, chasing, or willful disturbance since 1979, and they were assigned the status of "endangered" in 1983. Yet they keep dying.

There was concern that the St. Lawrence might be unfit for belugas as early as 1973. A calf killed by hunters in 1972 was found to contain very high concentrations of DDT and PCBs in its blubber. Lower levels of these substances have been associated with premature births and reproductive failure in California sea lions.

In the whales' main habitat, large quantities of PAHs were discovered, including BaP, a highly carcinogenic compound released by local smelting factories. (An increased frequency of urinary bladder tumors among aluminum workers from the area has also been attributed to BaP.) A study produced in 1987 stated that these chemicals have contaminated the beluga food web, producing disease and deformity in the whales.

How can a mammal the size of a whale be fatally injured by a chemical? A food chain "domino effect" occurs when animals that naturally prey on each other unwittingly ingest persistent toxins that have accumulated in their victim's bodies. In the Great Lakes, PCB contamination is particularly prevalent. First, PCBs enter the ecosystem—through old, leaking appliances, for example.

Above: ***Cosmos, a double-crested cormorant, was found on an island in Lake Michigan in 1988. His twisted, deformed bill was caused by PCB poisoning. Dr. James Ludwig has chronicled the increase of deformities in cormorants due to pollution.***

They are carried into sewers and streams, which bring them to the lakes. There they attach themselves to small particles in the water, and settle at the bottom, where mayflies, midges, and worms feed on them. Fish then consume the mud-dwelling organisms. The PCBs are stored in the fat of the fish; over its lifetime, trace amounts ingested daily can add up tremendously. The gull, mink, or larger fish that eats the smaller one then acquires that smaller one's accumulation of PCBs. A human eating the larger fish gets the total load of PCBs it amassed while it was alive. If a nursing mother eats the fish, the highest concentration of the chemicals is transferred to her newborn child.

Snapping turtles collected from Great Lakes waters have exhibited deformities and reproductive problems. Large, very old turtles that lived in the sediment on the bottom of lakes in the basin proved to be very contaminated. One turtle from Hamilton, Ontario, contained 2,097 ppm of PCBs. (The U.S. Food and Drug Administration deems poultry with 3 ppm of PCBs unfit for human consumption.)

Clearly, if the benthic organisms—the bottom-dwelling worms, insects, mollusks, and plankton—are assaulted with toxic chemicals, the pollution will echo all the way up the food chain, from fish to turtles and fish-eating birds, reptiles, mammals, and humans. In the richest estuaries on Lake Michigan, such as Green Bay and the mouth of the Fox River, benthic populations have been saturated with chemical waste. These two locations are heavily contaminated with lead, mercury, oil, grease, PCBs, zinc, and DDT. Bullhead catfish from this region show tumors; fish-eating birds are born with defects.

In 1985, more than four million anglers fished on the Great Lakes. Economically, the region gained over a billion U.S. dollars and more than three million Canadian dollars from sport fishing.

But, in 1983, the Canadian government acknowledged that, "Fish, particularly from the Great Lakes, represent the most serious identified source of dioxins in human food." A recent study by the National Wildlife Federation concluded that eating as few as 11 meals in a lifetime of the largest, most contaminated fish from Lake Michigan will significantly increase the risk of cancer. Greenpeace pronounced that the flesh of many Great Lakes fish is tainted with a broad range of contaminants, including PCBs, pesticides, dioxins, and heavy metals. Many species have various types of cancer; in some locations, 100 percent of the species sampled had cancer.

At Wayne State University in Michigan, researchers found that infants whose mothers had eaten PCB-contaminated fish were shorter and weighed less at birth. These babies also had smaller heads and displayed obvious abnormalities in their behavior and in their neuromuscular systems. The more contaminated fish consumed by the mother, the greater the abnormalities visible in her offspring.

The nature of PCBs makes them so long-lasting that they are passed from mother to child during pregnancy and through breast feeding. Thus, measurable amounts of the chemical will still be evident in children five generations later, even if no new exposure to PCBs occurs.

Sport fish consumption warnings are in effect in every one of the lakes. Toxic contamination is present throughout the waters of the basin; fish in all five lakes and their connecting channels have

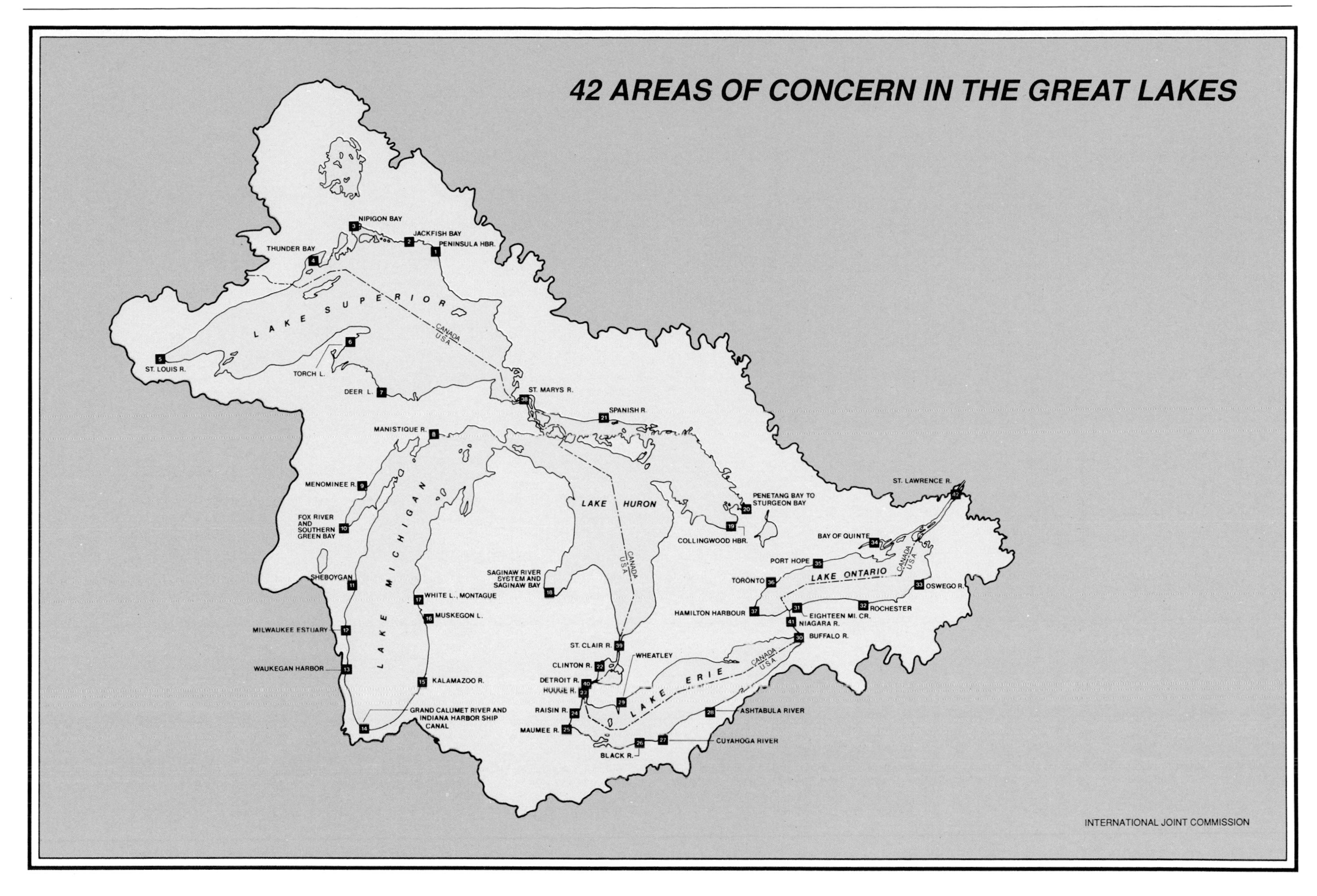

Above: ***The forty-two Areas of Concern in the Great Lakes region. Contamination of all but one of the sites is due to toxic pollution.***

been found with tumors, cancers, lesions, and deformities. Recently, 80 percent of bullheads three years old and older were found to have liver tumors in a polluted tributary of Lake Erie, Ohio's Black River. One hundred percent of carp and a hybrid species of goldfish collected from Detroit's Rouge River showed tumors in the sex organs of adult males. In Torch Lake, a contaminated waterway leading to Lake Superior, all of the sauger in a small sample were diagnosed with liver tumors. Currently, Superior is the only one of the Great Lakes where trout are able to reproduce.

Although Lake Ontario is the most polluted of the five, Lake Michigan has the greatest number of AOCs. The only lake that lies entirely within the United States, its shoreline is besieged by 10 heavily polluted sites. The degradation affecting Michigan is attributed to the dumping of industrial and municipal waste water, runoff from city streets and farm fields, tainted river and harbor sediments, adulterated ground water, and air pollution.

© Jeff Kaufman/FPG International

Agreement (GLWQA). Two key principles were adopted. First, the Great Lakes basin was recognized as an "ecosystem"—i.e., the air, land, water, and living organisms, including humans, were viewed as interacting components of one system; and, second, the "virtual elimination of persistent toxic substances" was suggested through a regulatory philosophy of "zero discharge."

During the 1980s, the Reagan Administration repeatedly threatened the elimination of Great Lakes research programs. Congress was able to save them; however, their funding levels were markedly reduced.

The visionary principles affirmed in the GLWQA of 1978 were renewed and expanded in 1987. Yet, they endure as principles only, because none of the existing governing bodies in the basin have passed them into laws. Time is passing, and the dumping of toxic chemicals continues.

Despite the fact that some fish species have made comebacks and the Cuyahoga River is not flowing with more chemicals than water, the Great Lakes ecosystem remains threatened. Forty years have passed since the dramatic influx of chemicals began. It was 25 years ago that scientists realized toxic waste was poisoning the fish and wildlife. Yet during all of this time, the Great Lakes ecosystem has not been protected from further deterioration, and the prospects of restoring it completely do not look bright.

Far left: ***Before cleanup of toxics can begin, the contents of these barrels must be tested to see what they contain.*** **Above:** ***Barrels stored outside eventually corrode, and their contents spill or are washed onto the ground by rain.*** **Left:** ***Water ripples over a sandbar near a pristine Lake Michigan beach. The beauty of this scene may soon be marred by continuing pollution of the air and water.***

AIRBORNE POLLUTANTS

Further delay in action to help the Great Lakes arises from the continued operations of industry. Airborne pollutants from within the basin—and from continents away—pass over the lakes and settle in them. Air pollution originating in St. Louis, Pittsburgh, and Newfoundland can reach the basin in five days.

Atmospheric pollution to the lakes is so widespread that almost all the contamination reaching them from PCBs, DDT, BaP, and lead is carried through the air. Each of the lakes is so laden with PCBs that they themselves have become a source of the toxic compounds; PCBs are released from surface waters through evaporation. Sadly, and ironically, Lake Michigan is now the largest source of PCBs that infiltrates Lake Superior.

Wind currents are capable of blowing pollutants around the world in only two to three weeks. Pollution from major midwestern American cities like St. Louis, Chicago, and Minneapolis falls over the Great Lakes in less than seven days' time. Additionally, the lakes bear the brunt of toxic chemicals that are transported from Third World countries, where they are used regularly, even though they are banned in North America. Therefore, regardless of what individual gains are made throughout the lakes, basin residents and wildlife are constantly contending with a serious air pollution problem.

The Sierra Club, Citizens for a Better Environment, Great Lakes United, and Lake Michigan Federation have named the incineration of garbage as one of the major contributors to air pollution and environmental degradation in the lakes. They declared that if the 300 proposed incinerator facilities are indeed built in the United States in the next few years, new lead emissions could affect reductions already achieved through auto emission controls. The incineration of domestic and chemical wastes is extensive in the basin, and creates dioxins and furans in the atmosphere. Indeed, incineration is the major source of these poisons. But incinerators also spew heavy metals, like mercury, which is toxic to the nervous system. Of the 42 AOCs, mercury pollution is noted in 33 areas and has been designated a problem in 18 of the sites.

In the St. Louis River, increased mercury concentrations are being attributed to the incineration of garbage, which began in the late 1980s. Before that time, municipal refuse was landfilled and sewage sludge was applied on the land. Incineration has since become popular as a sludge disposal method, and this process operates in 22 of the AOCs. In the Lower Fox River/Green Bay tributary to Lake Michigan, sediment concentrations of mercury have increased 45 percent over the last ten years.

The world's largest trash incinerator is located in downtown Detroit, Michigan; the plant burns 4,000 tons (3,600 metric tons) of garbage every day. A year before it went "on-line," Greenpeace warned that it would pose a cancer risk to the people of Detroit 19 times higher than anything previously licensed in Michigan. They projected that it would shoot more than 2,000 tons (1,800 metric tons) of toxic gases and particles across the Detroit River every day.

© Howard G. Ross/FPG International

The town of Pripayat will be uninhabitable for over 20,000 years due to the contamination caused by the explosion at Chernobyl.

Previous page: ***The Great Lakes are extremely sensitive to air pollution, from smokestacks in the basin as well as emissions hundreds of miles away.***

The plant began burning on a test basis late in 1989. A few weeks later, construction workers walked off their jobs due to health complaints that included skin rashes, swelling of the hands, eye irritation, coughing spells, and shortness of breath. Samples of ash smuggled to Greenpeace were tested and found to contain extremely high levels of lead, cadmium, and other dangerous substances.

In the Great Lakes basin, dozens of garbage incinerators are being proposed as alternatives to diminishing landfill space. But for every three tons (2.7 metric tons) of trash burned, one ton (.9 metric ton) of extremely toxic ash is created—which has to be landfilled. Particles that fly from the stack proceed in a plume across residential tracts, farms, and water resources. Greenpeace has alerted the public that incineration takes our garbage and turns it into a health hazard.

Greenpeace, the National Wildlife Federation, and the Canadian Institute for Environmental Policy and Law have responded to the Great Lakes' peril by calling for a program of "zero discharge" at once. They demand that all sources of toxic pollution, whether they are discharged into air, water, or onto land, be controlled and eventually eliminated. All water quality standards and objectives for persistent toxic substances must be zero. A "toxics freeze" would immediately prohibit any further infusion of toxics into the Great Lakes.

Above left: ***This turtle's pond and shell are covered with an algal scum, probably indicating an unclean habitat.*** **Above right:** ***This rock formation rests on the shores of Lake Michigan, where pollution threatens to destroy vulnerable ecosystems.***

Though the peoples of the world inhabit various countries, we are, after all, citizens of a global community. We must share air, water, and land. These components are necessary for the survival of all of us, which makes the health of each one of us important to all.

Much of the food we eat is grown on soils thousands of miles from our supermarkets. Thus, pesticides and fertilizers applied in distant fields do affect us. And nowhere is the connection between the natural systems of the earth and its inhabitants more evident than in the microcosm of the Great Lakes basin.

We know from the atmospheric testing of nuclear weapons and the Chernobyl incident that contaminants are rapidly transported around the globe. Smokestacks in the American midwest are a major contributor to acid rain in the northeast. Like a bull's-eye in a target, the Great Lakes not only absorb pollution from the farm field runoff and industrial cities surrounding them, but from wind currents that carry toxins from Mexico and Central America. They are a telling case for the global control of toxic chemical production.

Pollution has reached a sufficient level that nothing less than a worldwide ban on the manufacture, transport, and use of dangerous chemicals will "cure" the Great Lakes. Without it, the contamination of this marvelous ecosystem will continue indefinitely.

At home in the sun-filtered depths of tropical rain forests are animals, plants, and insects that defy imagination. The transparent skin of a "glass" frog no more than one inch (2.5 cm) long reveals green bones and a straight red vein connected to the heart. A "fragrant butterfly" mimics the scent and color of chocolate. Butterflies with wings of electric blue and moths with a wingspan of nearly one foot (30 cm) dart and hover among the leaves and flowers. Orchid blossoms the size of an outstretched hand droop gracefully amid lush fronds. Some spiders are large enough to eat small birds that become trapped in their webs. Flying parrots, toucans, and macaws splash riotous colors against the jade green palette of the forest. Monkeys swing from the vines.

Perhaps two-thirds of the species that dwell in the tropical jungles spend their lives in the treetops. They never venture to the ground, even for reproduction. Endlessly bridging the "arboreal gap" are the stinging ants, scorpions, and wasps that scale the barks and branches of trees. The forest floor is the realm of the insects. Swarms of ants, beetles, and termites trample fallen vegetation, consuming it, carrying it away or otherwise helping it to rapidly decompose.

Here, in the luxurious equatorial belt girdling the globe, reside as many as one-half of *all* earth's life forms. It is the most diverse of any major ecosystem on the earth, due to the region's perennial climate of high temperatures and generous rainfall. About 13 to 26 feet (4 to 8 m) of rain are recorded per year in the tropic zone. Borneo receives an average of 16 feet (5 m) per year, which is five times the amount of rain that falls on New York.

Although these torrential rains descend at least once a day, they are blocked by masses of treetops, tangling vines, and leaves. Water rolls down limbs and trunks to the forest floor, while a fine spray of moisture drips constantly from leaf tips, maintaining a humid hothouse climate in which plants thrive.

There is no dry or cold season to inhibit growth in the rain forest. It is in the heavy vegetation where four-fifths of the rain forests' nutrients are located. Tropical forest soils are virtually sterile because only the first few inches contain small amounts of nutrients.

Just seven percent of the land mass, or two percent of the earth's surface, is covered by tropical rain forests. Originally, their verdant belt of green spanned twice that area. About 2.4 million acres (1 million ha) remain in a 3,000-mile- (4,800-km-) wide band that circles the equator. The major stands that are left are located in Amazonia (Brazil), Southeast Asia, and West Africa. About a third of existing tropical forests are in Brazil; Indonesia and Zaire also support some rain forests.

The richness of this comparatively small ecosystem cannot be underestimated. A majority of the world's known life forms—plants, animals, insects—are found only in the rain forests, and scientists estimate that many more undiscovered species may be found there in the future. Of the 250,000 identified plant species in the world today, 90,000 live in the rain forest. At least another 30,000 plants, most of which are also in the jungle, wait to be discovered.

According to Rainforest Action Network, a typical four-square-mile (10-km^2) patch of rain forest harbors as many as 1,500 species of flowering plants, 750 species of trees, 125 mammal species, 400 bird species, 100 reptile species, 60 amphibian species, and 150 butterfly species. A

Far left: ***Iguaçú Falls in Brazil. Lush, dense jungle growth is characteristic of a tropical rain forest.*** **Above:** ***From a rain forest in Malaysia, the*** **Phyllium pulchrifolium** ***is an insect that strongly resembles the leaves on this branch.***

© Karl Weidmann/Valan Photos

This Venezuelan tamandua, an arboreal anteater, could not survive the destruction of its tree-filled habitat.

FOREST RELATIONSHIPS

In a tropical rain forest, plant and animal life is "layered." Tall trees, ranging in height from 100 to 200 feet (30 to 60 meters) are at the highest level. Their crowns form an umbrella over the forest, shading it. Although sunlight can enter, it is much dimmed, as if it were penetrating an intricately laced curtain. This lack of sunlight discourages dense growth on the forest floor.

Thick, wood-tough vines called lianas dominate the layer below the top canopy of trees. They hang entwined from branches, which are also encrusted with *epiphytes*. Epiphytes, or air plants, and lianas use the trees for physical support, but they do not act in a parasitic way upon them. This group of plants includes ferns, mosses, lichens, liverworts, arboreal cacti, and bromeliads. The epiphytes, having no underground roots, derive their nourishment from the environment around them. Minerals are acquired from falling leaves and wastes of animals. Bromeliads, which are related to the pineapple, store rainwater at the base of their leaves, like other air plants. These elevated pools teem with microcommunities of frogs, insects, and spiders.

Orchids are probably the most familiar of the epiphytes. Over 20,000 species of this exotic flower are known, and most of them hang on the upper trunks and branches of tropic trees. More than 1,100 varieties of orchids have been identified in Costa Rica alone.

Smaller trees that receive less sunlight, and so stretch from 30 to 90 feet (9 to 27 m) high, fill in the gap between the ground and the crowns of the highest rain forest trees.

Opossums, lemurs, sloths, monkeys, and other mammals inhabit the treetops of the jungle. Macaws, smaller parrots, bats, and other brilliant avian creatures fly from limb to limb. Insects, frogs, snakes, and fungi coat the lower levels of the trees, and the forest floor.

One-fifth of all the plants and birds on earth evolved in the Amazon basin. The tropics are the planet's oldest continuous ecosystem. Fossils reveal that the forests of Southeast Asia have endured in basically their present form for 70 to 100 million years. The constant humid climate lasting throughout that span of time made possible the growth of a "species bank"—a veritable storehouse of genetic diversity in the rain forests.

Amazing, too, are the symbiotic relationships that have developed among the jungle's flora and fauna, the specialized co-evolution of species that ensures survival for all. Some plants exude the odor of rotting meat in order to attract flies for pollination. Trees depend on fish to spread their seeds when the rivers flood. A particular kind of wasp is nourished by a fig tree; the tree, in turn, is pollinated by the wasp. The shape of one species of orchid resembles a female insect. When the male insect attempts to copulate with the orchid, the seed is fertilized.

The system of reciprocity is exemplified by the relationship between the acacia tree and the ants that live on it. Without the ants, the tree would die. On the underside of the tree's thorns are holes bored by the ants, where they live. Ants harvest the leaf tips—a source of vitamins and oils—for their larvae. In return for the use of the tree as a home and provider of food, the ants attack any other creatures on it, stinging their victims and protecting the tree.

© B. Lyon/Valan Photos

© Anne Heimann

© D. Long/Envision

Left: ***A silky waterfall descends through the depths of this Guatemalan forest.*** **Top:** ***The poison dart frog,*** **Dendrobates pumilio,** ***of Costa Rica.*** **Above:** ***A cluster of unidentified orchids, a type of Phaleanopsis.***

Just as incredible as the life forms of the tropics and the mutual dependencies they have established is the rate at which the ecosystem is being obliterated. Since 1960, more than a quarter of all Central American forests have been destroyed to raise beef, 85 to 95 percent of which was exported to the United States. Although this represents less than two percent of total U.S. beef consumption, it has had a devastating effect on Central American forests. The nutrient-depleted soil can barely achieve 50 pounds (22 kg) meat production per acre per year. Not only cattle ranching, but also farming and cutting trees for fuel have thinned Central and South American forests. In Africa and Madagascar, as well as South and Southeast Asia, farming, logging, and fuel wood consumption have endangered the rain forest habitat and the planet.

All of the primary rain forests in India, Sri Lanka, and Bangladesh have been razed. The Ivory Coast forests are nearly completely logged. The Philippines lost more than half their rain forest between 1960 and 1985; Thailand leveled almost half during the same period.

Every year at least 50 million more acres (20 million ha) of rain forest are decimated. That amount equals the land mass of England, Scotland, and Wales.

Unless the deforestation is halted immediately, all Malaysian peninsular rain forests will be gone this year. By the year 2000, Nigeria could be deforested; Thailand and the Congo are slated for 60 to 68 percent jungle removal each. Likewise, Guatemala, Colombia, Guinea, and Madagascar will have lost a third of their tropic cover by 2000; Ghana will have demolished one quarter of its rain forest. Honduras, Nicaragua, and Ecuador will have erased half of their remaining forests by the end of the century.

In 10 years, rain forests in Central America, Southeast Asia, West Africa, the Himalayan foothills, and the Pacific Islands will have largely disappeared. Brazil will be minus an area of rain forest that is more than twice the size of Portugal. To date, we have flattened more than half of the world's tropic trees. With every ancient tree that is felled, we deny ourselves and generations of the future the wealth of benefits that are supplied by the rain forests and no other ecosystem.

Consider how closely we interact in our everyday lives with products derived from the equatorial zone. How many of these spices are on your shelf? Allspice, black pepper, cardamom, cayenne, chili, cinnamon, cloves, ginger, nutmeg, paprika, sesame seeds, vanilla. . . all originate in the rain forests. Are you fond of Brazil nuts? Chocolate? Coffee? Your cupboard is probably stocked with cane sugar, peanuts, cola drinks, and tea. Cashews and macadamias, cucumbers, peppers, and tapioca—all of these food items are from the rain forests, as is much of the fruit that you buy at the market—apples, avocados, oranges, grapefruit, eggplants, lemons, bananas, coconuts, limes, papayas, pineapples, and tangerines are only some of the fruits that are harvested from the tropics!

Advances in agriculture have succeeded with the aid of rain forest plants and insects. Crop breeders require genes from wild plants and primitive crops to fortify modern strains. Every modern rice plant contains the gene resistant to grassy stunt virus, a major rice disease. That gene was discovered just 25 years ago and was found in only two minute seeds from central India. No other seeds containing the resistant gene were ever found again.

The rosy periwinkle,* Catharanthus roseus, *offers sufferers of lymphocytic leukemia and Hodgkin's disease a chance of recovery.

Previous page: *Severe erosion follows in the wake of tropical forest removal in Madagascar.*

Fruit and vegetable types from rain forests, when crossed with modern produce strains, have resulted in improvements that translate to millions of dollars in increased annual farm revenues. Imported insects are efficient biological pest controls; in Florida, three types of parasitic wasps save citrus growers $30 million annually in crop damage. Tomato varieties have been improved by cross-breeding with wild tomatoes from Ecuador, Chile, and Peru, resulting in an additional five million dollars in farm revenue per year.

Many other rain forest plants have the potential of becoming global food staples as their properties are explored.

Dramatic strides in modern medical science are also greatly due to ingredients from the tropics. The National Cancer Institute divulged that 70 percent of all the plants identified as having anti-cancer qualities occur only in the rain forests. In Costa Rica, 225 plants are documented as promising anti-cancer agents.

Centuries-old ipecac, from South America, is still the most effective treatment for amoebic dysentery. Morphine originates from the poppy tree, and quinine from the cinchona tree. People afflicted with lymphocytic leukemia have a 90 percent chance of remission thanks to the rosy periwinkle. Its leaves are used in the medication vincristine; annual sales worldwide exceed $50 million. The same plant offers Hodgkin's disease sufferers a significant chance of recovery.

The West African Calabar bean is used as a remedy for glaucoma. A vine from the same area provides the basis for strophanthin, a heart medicine. Reserpine, from India and Southeast Asia, is considered essential for treating hypertension. Cortisone and diosgenin are extracted from wild yams of Mexico and Guatemala. Diosgenin is ranked as the most versatile and available steroid raw material, and is an active ingredient in oral contraceptives.

Curare, a derivative of a South American tree bark, cannot be chemically synthesized in a laboratory. Many delicate surgical operations, such as tonsillectomies and abdominal procedures, would be enormously difficult without curare, which relaxes skeletal muscles.

For a Third World country like India, the annual gain from exporting resins, rattans, flowers, essential oils, perfumes, and flavorings—all products of the rain forests—is $125 million.

Thaumatin, from West Africa's katemfe bush, is a newly discovered compound that reigns as the sweetest substance in the world. It is 100,000 times sweeter than table sugar! Another recent find was a wild coffee plant that has no caffeine.

Astonishingly, the sap of an Amazonian tree, the copaiba, is nearly identical to diesel fuel. Poured straight into a fuel tank, it can power a truck. In 1975, it was discovered that oil drawn from the jojoba bean could perform as a high-grade industrial fluid. Because it is also similar to sperm whale oil, widespread use of the jojoba could help save the whales.

As miraculous as the assets of tropical rain forest plants are, less than one percent of them have been thoroughly examined for their chemical compounds. Although jungles contain more organisms than any other land ecosystem, fewer individuals of any one species reside in a given area. For example, a hectare of forest in Central America may support 200 different species of trees, but perhaps only two exist of the same species. When a section of jungle is cleared, the bulldozer is the only beneficiary of plants that could have transformed the world of the future. These medicinal and nutritional substances may never be encountered again.

With their habitat uprooted, the rate of survival for many unique species appears bleak. As greater areas of jungle are turned into bare patches of soil, the jaguars, anteaters, arrow-poison frogs, and toucans that lived there will find it harder to reproduce. Their realm will be reduced to only those forest areas left on steep slopes or in ravines, where it is impractical to clear.

The situation is drastic in Madagascar, an island about twice the size of Arizona that lies 250 miles (400 km) off Africa's east coast. Eighty percent of the plant and animal populations of the island are endemic—that is, they exist nowhere else in the world. Nearly 80 percent of the 8,500 species of plants on Madagascar grow there only. Lemurs, one of the major groups of primates, survive exclusively on this island. Indeed, five percent of the total amount of diversity on the planet is located on this small island.

In 1949, 66 percent of the original rain forest cover was left on Madagascar. By 1984, it had dropped by half. Today, less than one-tenth of the country's land surface still supports natural vegetation. The terrible loss of species that has accompanied the destruction of this habitat can only be imagined. People may wonder what difference it makes whether there's one species or 10 species

The Cinchona tree, source of quinine, native to the tropical rain forests.

less in some tropical forest. The answer is that although it may be difficult to quantify the exact worth of an individual species, each species makes an incremental and essential contribution to maintaining the stability of global chemistry and climate.

In 1987 one study surmised that since the forests where at least half the earth's 2.2 million species occur will very probably be reduced to less than one-tenth of their total extent over the next 15 years or so, over a million species will become extinct during this period or soon afterwards. In western Ecuador, for example, a region that was almost completely forested as recently as 1950 is now almost completely deforested. As extensive deforestation of this kind spreads in many other regions, the rate of extinction will average more than 100 species a day, with the rate increasing from perhaps a few species a day now to several hundred by the early years of the next century. The great majority of these will not have been collected, and therefore will never be represented in any scientific collection, preserved, or known in any way. No comparable rate of extinction has occurred since the end of the Cretaceous Period, 65 million years ago, when more than half of the species on earth, including the dinosaurs, vanished.

If the destruction continues, many millions of years of plant and animal evolution will be permanently dismissed within a few decades. Of Ecuador's 700 known species of reptiles and amphibians, close to 200 have been discovered only since 1970. Perhaps at least three million tropical organisms worldwide have yet to be found and named. Some scientists believe the number may actually be 10 times higher.

At the very least, the thrill of encountering and studying the highly adapted creatures of the rain forest will be forever lost from human experience. Scientifically, we are losing the opportunity to understand the nature of much of the diversity of life on earth; aesthetically, we will be unable to appreciate the results of an uninterrupted path of evolution over the billions of years since life appeared on the planet; economically, we are denying ourselves, our children, and our grandchildren the opportunity to utilize many of the plants, animals, and microorganisms that can benefit our lives.

Planetary evolution has been forever influenced by the species loss in the tropical rain forest. Indeed, humanity may have permanently diverted the process of evolution, because the reduced pockets of jungle that remain cannot play the same role their ancestors once performed in their abundance. Biodiversity, the physical and biological complexity of an environment, maintains ecosystem stability. It also fosters a rich gene pool from the multitude of species that have evolved with their own genetic codes. A single plant can have 400,000 or more different genes. Just one gene could lead scientists to medical cures. Once a species is gone, however, so is its unique genetic coding.

Dead trees north of Alta Floresta, Brazil. Shallow rain forest soils are easily disturbed.

Slash and burn agriculture, here south of Santarem, Brazil, destroys thousands of acres of tropical forest.

RAIN FORESTS AND THE GLOBAL BALANCE OF NATURE

The wonders of the rain forests do not end with their overflowing bank of plant, animal, and insect life. They fulfill other necessary functions that relate to the overall balance of the earth.

Rain forests protect the watersheds that are directly connected to the survival of 40 percent of the world's farms. A watershed that is well-forested can trap 95 percent of the yearly rainfall in plant and tree roots. This prevents flooding and enables the roots to release their water gradually, which keeps streams running. Without the tropical rain forests, nations like Bangladesh would be caught in a destructive cycle of flood and drought.

Rainfall patterns are linked with the processes of the tropic jungles. About half of the rainwater that descends on the forests is returned to the atmosphere via evapotranspiration, a process that transfers water into the atmosphere from soil and the leaves of living plants. From this movement is created a great cloud of moisture that hovers over the forests. Carried by the wind, the moisture falls as rain thousands of miles distant. More than one-half of Amazonia's total annual rainfall is recycled in the direction of prevailing winds.

Evapotranspiration also absorbs large amounts of heat. Felled trees, conversely, lead to parched soils and dry air. If the cleared area is extensive enough, entire regions—once lush and wet—can suffer from lack of water.

Deforestation is already disrupting rainfall patterns; as the loss of trees increases, consequences are expected to be felt thousands of miles beyond the limits of the equatorial belt. Some tropical systems, like the Amazon, are currently experiencing an impaired capacity to recycle rainwater inland. Central Panama, which is deforested, has had an average annual rainfall drop of 17 inches (42 cm) in the last 50 years. The drought that has afflicted Africa for the past two decades may also be caused by the denuding of the tropics. In India, deforestation since 1950 has doubled the area affected by yearly floods. Six billion tons (5.4 billion metric tons) of soil are washed from the hills every year; many thousands of people are left homeless.

Because rain forests store vast reserves of carbon in their vegetation, burning them releases significant amounts of carbon dioxide into the atmosphere. Trees that are cut and left to decay also release carbon dioxide, but at a slower rate. Annually, fossil fuel combustion unleashes two to five times as much carbon as deforestation. Yet, the burning of tropical forests has been cited as the second largest factor contributing to the greenhouse effect.

Over the next 20 years, the earth could very well lose 40 percent of its biodiversity due to the rapid climate changes projected. These changes are being induced at such a rate that plants will probably not have time to adapt to them. In Southeast Asia, eons-old climatic patterns are being altered by removal of rain forests. More dramatic changes aggravated by global warming would threaten the region's worldwide exports of cocoa, tea, coffee, rubber, palm oil, spices, sugar cane, coconut, and other products.

© David L. Pearson/Visuals Unlimited

Rain forest destruction in South America. This patch has been cleared for an oil well.

Leveling the evergreen forests in South America would cause a regional temperature rise of 5 to 9° F (3 to 5° C). The dry season would be extended and the deterioration of remaining forests would hasten. These major changes will have a worldwide effect, although it is impossible to predict precisely what will happen.

It has been suggested that planting 325 million acres (130 million ha) of trees in developing countries and 100 million acres (40 million ha) of trees in industrial countries could conceivably reduce worldwide carbon emissions by a quarter of current levels. Such an effort would slow the

AMAZONIA

Amazonia is a pivotal environment because fully one-third of all tropical forests left on the planet are in Brazil, which owns half of the Amazon Basin.

Amazonia, embracing the Amazon River and the forest that buttresses it, covers 2.7 million square miles (7 million square km)—an area almost the size of the continental United States. Eight countries besides Brazil share the majesty of the mighty Amazon as it churns from the Andes to the Atlantic. Snaking its way for 4,000 miles (6,400 km), the Amazon is the widest river on earth, and only 100 miles (160 km) shorter in length than the Nile. Over 1,000 tributaries feed it; two-thirds of all the planet's river water saturate the Basin. Half of all the oxygen produced by the land plants in the world emerges from Amazonia. Every hour, the Amazon River pours an average of 170 billion gallons (646 billion l) of water into the Atlantic.

In this colossal ecosystem, lily pads form floating carpets three feet (.9 m) across. Some of the 500 species of catfish are so large it is claimed they have eaten children. One species actually walks along the ground on its fins! A certain type of top-dwelling minnow sports two sets of eyes—one pair sees above the water, and one pair sees below. Some of the 40 species of electric eels in the Amazon can jolt their prey with 800 volts of electricity. The bald uakari monkey has a hairless forehead; its pink face turns purple when it becomes excited. Butterflies with a wingspan of eight inches (20 cm) flit across the jungle. Fungi break down plant matter so quickly that the roots of living plants obtain nutrients in six weeks.

In 1987 alone, Brazil burned an area almost the size of Austria. But in 1989, increased governmental controls and inspection caused a significant drop in rain forest destruction to 30 percent less than the previous year. The Brazilian Institute of Environment and Renewable Natural Resources, founded in 1989 in response to the outcry against further forest clearing, supervised 612 rangers in a region half the size of Europe. This crew was able to target locations of illegal burnings, fine the guilty parties, and remove officials who protected landowners destroying the trees.

The president of the organization, Fernando Cesar Mesquita, felt that even more forest could have been saved if the developed countries he had asked for help—the United States, France, Britain, Italy, and West Germany—had supplied aid for ecological protection. Mr. Mesquita was only able to obtain five helicopters with the help of the Brazilian government. He had requested radar-mapping equipment, patrol boats, four-wheel drive vehicles, telecommunications paraphernalia, and more helicopters from the other nations. It is not easy to carry out the measures necessary to preserve the forests when inspectors for the Institute are intimidated, shot at—or even killed, as in the case of one member.

Mr. Mesquita emphasized that Brazil bears the highest foreign debt of any country in the developing world—$110 billion—and that he supports debt-for-ecology swaps. To date, he has not received any offers.

Far left: ***The jade green shoreline of the Lower Amazon River in Brazil.*** **Above:** ***The*** **Agrias narcissus** ***butterfly of Brazil, one of dozens of richly hued insects existing in the tropics.***

© Michael Major/Envision

Above: ***New plantain growth sprouts on stripped tropical soil. Once rain forests have been cleared, it is impossible to replace the diversity of plants, trees, insects, and animals that once crowded this delicate ecosystem.*** **Right:** ***Will this North Sumatra rain forest survive?***

GLOBAL ACTION

Other buds of hope for the rain forest are blossoming around the world. In Kenya, the National Council of Women is sponsoring the Greenbelt Movement. They have mobilized over 15,000 farmers and half a million students to plant more than two million trees. The American Forestry Association has spearheaded a campaign to plant 100 million trees across the United States by 1992.

In 1985, the Tropical Forestry Action Plan was launched by the U.N. Development Program, World Resources Institute, the Food/Agriculture Organization, and the World Bank. The first steps toward an aggressive tree-planting effort and forest protection plan were taken.

Two years later, the first Central American Environmental Action Conference was held. As a result, a declaration was issued by representatives of the six Central American nations that participated. In part, it read, "If the process of environmental deterioration continues, it will make future development impossible and it will deepen social instability. Given this, we must search for a new development path. In order to guarantee sustainable development, we must gain social and economic justice by diversifying production and raising the standard of living, and at the same time, harmonize human actions with nature.

"The representatives and delegates of this Conference have decided to organize themselves into a regional network for environmental action. The network will coordinate the implementation of our recommendations and convert them into action for peace and sustainable development. . ."

Humans are striving to repair the damage that has been wrought on the planet's most invaluable ecosystem. Locked in the fronds of the jungle are the seeds of our evolutionary past, and the stepping stones to a stable future. What secrets do the trees still hold? Perhaps we already know the most important one: Humanity needs the tropical rain forests.

THE AFRICAN SAHEL

Overgrazing by large herds of animals removes vegetation. These goats leave dust in their wake.

DESERTIFICATION

Worsening these problems is an ecological process called desertification, which occurs on land that has been misused. Finer particles of soil are blown or washed away, leaving coarse sand in their place. In the Sahel, 50 years of deforestation and the overgrazing of cattle have allowed the desert to fill in a previously green area the size of France and Austria.

Desertification is not unique to Africa; yearly, 27,000 square miles (70,000 square km) across the globe are lost to the progression of desert. But in the Sahelian zone countries, desertification is proceeding at a rate seven times the Third World average! In one country alone, Mali, the Sahara has been drawn 210 miles (350 km) farther south in the last 20 years.

Nature is constantly fabricating new topsoil, at her own pace of 1.5 tons per year (3.4 metric tons). However, human activities, including removal of vegetation, overgrazing of cattle, and lack of prudent soil conservation practices, lead to the direct expansion of the desert, because topsoil is being dislodged faster than nature can replace it. In recent years, the difference between the loss and creation of new topsoil has grown rapidly. Dust crossing the Atlantic has been measured at Barbados in the West Indies, where its accumulations have risen drastically in the last two decades. The origin of the "dust" was the African Sahel; it was actually topsoil blown across the ocean.

Why is desertification spreading so rampantly in the Sahel, when for centuries the entire continent was sustained by subsistence farming and herding? Indigenous African cultures had developed production systems that were well adapted to the limitations of the Sahel. "Shifting cultivation" and "bush fallow" agricultural methods allowed fields to rest and recover their nutrients and moisture for lengthy periods after two to three seasons of harvesting crops. Often, traditional systems of farming also integrated the raising of livestock with agriculture. Cattle and goats were fed on crop residues and tree fodder; their wastes were used as organic fertilizers for fields and gardens. In a similar fashion, pastoralists who live in drier Sahelian areas where farming is not productive maintained the balance of nature by moving their herds around in search of water and vegetation. However, these traditional subsistence methods have been increasingly disrupted by rapid population growth, changing social, political, and economic policies, and inappropriate Western-styled plans for development. These changes have disrupted the delicate balance that allowed the Sahelians and their environment to co-exist for so many years.

Africa has the highest annual population growth rate of any country in the world, yet food production is increasing at a much slower rate. The current population of 450 million in sub-Saharan Africa's 42 countries is expected to triple in four decades. The addition of so many more people to an inherently fragile environment could force a further decline in land productivity.

The highest mortality rates on the planet are also recorded in this troubled nation. Of the seven million deaths that occur in the world each year, five million are in Africa. The number of children born to each woman has not changed, but infant mortality has dropped—from 167 per thousand in 1960 to 122 per thousand, due to the intervention of Western health care.

Besides population, another factor contributes to extending the edges of the desert. The carrying capacity of the land—the amount of human and animal life it can support within its resource base—has often been exceeded in the Sahel. An extremely dry strip of rangeland immediately south of the

This area of the Namibian Desert in South West Africa is known as the Skeleton Coast.

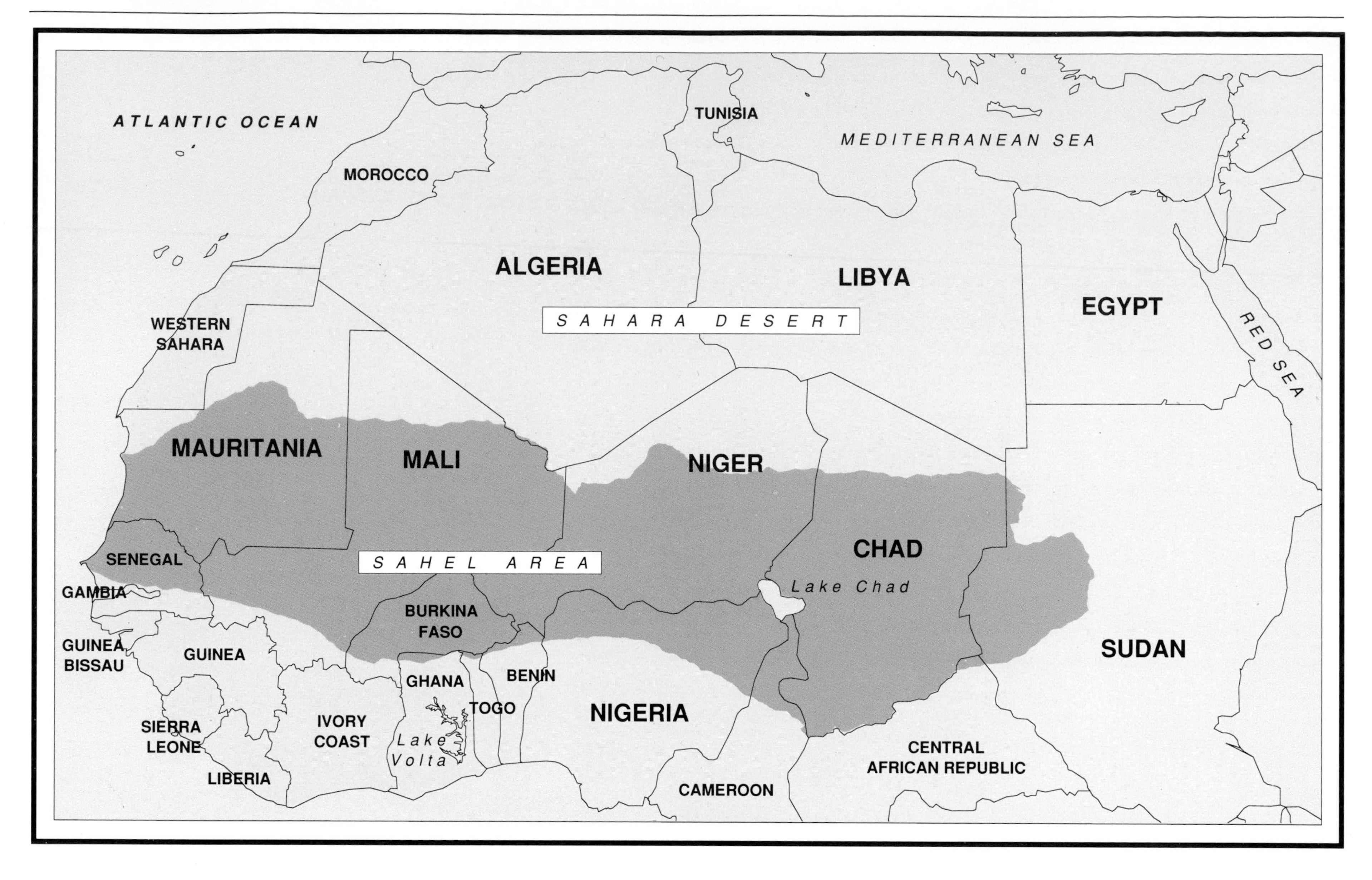

The Sahel region of Africa, one of the most severely afflicted desertified areas of the world.

Sahara can support 0.8 people per square mile, yet today, there are approximately five people trying to exist in this area. More to the south, where 14 to 24 inches (35 to 60 cm) of rain fall each year, 50 people per square mile live on land that can only support 37.

A study initiated by the World Bank focused on seven countries: Chad, Gambia, Burkina Faso, Mali, Niger, Mauritania, and Senegal. Across these land areas, rainfall increases from north to south. Likewise, the carrying capacity of their traditional farming and livestock methods parallels the amount of rainfall each region receives. In 1980, in two out of five east-west trending zones, the rural population required more food than the land could sustainably produce.

A similar study conducted by the United Nations Food and Agriculture Organization (FAO) found that 14 countries with a combined population of more than half that of sub-Saharan Africa had exceeded their carrying capacities in 1982. By 2000, seven more countries are expected to surpass their food carrying capacities.

In Mali, herdsmen bring their stock to a well for watering.

Africa's land is being overexploited not only by humans, but by livestock. Nomadic herding has proven to be an efficient way of harnessing the slim productivity potential of the Sahel. But in order for this type of herding to be fruitful, a delicate balance between the number of cattle or goats and the amount of vegetation they consume must be maintained. Too many animals trample or consume all plant growth, and then denude the trees. Without plant cover, the soil dries out in the extremely hot temperatures. Humus, the organic part of soil, is simply blown away. When rain falls, a crust is formed. The next rain, instead of seeping into the parched soil, flows across the earth. Baobab trees, unable to draw moisture from the ground, die. The cattle die—from starvation, not lack of water. The nomads, for whom cattle are wealth, move farther and farther south in search of new pasture. Behind them, a pox of cleared patches of land breaks out—land where trees have been cut so that people could farm and cattle graze. Eventually, the patches dehydrate until they merge in a further advance of desert. It is estimated that overcultivation and overgrazing lead to the widening of the Sahara by 40 to 90 miles (64 to 144 km) per year.

The process of desertification in Africa, goaded by cattle-ranching projects, is advancing beyond the Sahel even into regions where heavier rainfall normally creates lush vegetation. In Botswana, a nation in the highlands of southern Africa, an enormous cattle population is creating a desert wasteland from a vast savannah and wildlife ecosystem that until recently rivaled the richness of the Serengeti. Subsidized by the World Bank, three million cattle are roaming "ranges" that are actually the last untouched grasslands of the Kalahari Desert. A new program is invading the Okavango Delta, a huge swamp that shelters millions of migratory birds, plus elephants, antelopes, hippos, and a multitude of unique fish species. The nomadic Kalahari Bushmen, who lived in supreme harmony with this environment for generations, are also being displaced.

© Domenico Ruzza/Envision

These women probably walked many miles to collect their bundles of firewood. They need to replenish supplies daily for cooking and heating.

Under this $18 million livestock project, Botswana has lost its status as a net food exporter. Today, two-thirds of its one million inhabitants exist on food aid, most of which is shipped from the United States. In the midst of their food crisis, Botswana exports thousands of tons of beef to the European Economic Community, which is glutted with surplus meat. So Botswana's beef is resold, to the Soviet Union, for less than 10 percent of the cost of production. Soil productivity is being reduced as environmental degradation stretches across a once-healthy landscape. Food shortage, in turn, leads to famine and starvation—the same scenario being played out in the Sahel. Throughout Africa, sustainability is a precarious balancing act between the constraints of the ecosystem and methods of agriculture that do not exceed the threshold level of nature.

In a climate like the Sahel, trees play an invaluable role. Each one is an anchor that holds soil against gales of wind. Trees break the gusts, giving shelter and allowing vegetation to grow nearby. They cool the surface of the soil and provide nourishing humus after they decay. When seeds are planted, therefore, crops have a nutrient base from which to grow. For these reasons, the cutting of live trees is forbidden in the Sahel. However, the edict is largely ignored. Multitudes of people need to replenish wood daily for two very basic functions—cooking and heating. Eighty to 90 percent of the wood taken in the Sahel is used in these ways.

Women are responsible for collecting firewood, and often spend half a day or longer scavenging kindling. As more and more trees are uprooted, they must move farther and farther away from their homes to search. Outings of five or 10 miles (8 or 16 km) each day are not uncommon. When they collect enough logs, stumps, and twigs, they return to grind the millet and cook the food. Farming is

© Tim Gibson/Envision

In Niger, a village is viewed through the haze of a dust storm.

their responsibility; along with the rest of their nation, they grow 80 percent of the food their families eat. Women also rear the children, who help them collect water.

Though it is their work that forms the crux of Africa's agrarian economy, women are mostly excluded from access to loans, education, and extension services. At the same time, environmental degradation has intensified their workload. World Watch Institute added that because women are unable to enhance the productivity of their plots, they suffer along with their families, who depend on them for sustenance.

There is an endless quest for fuel to enable cooking and heating for another day. Dung, traditionally used to fertilize crops, is not being returned to the soil, but has become a substitute for scarce firewood. The soil is rapidly depleted, since the nitrogen, phosphorus, and other nutrients contained in the dung are no longer being supplied. As a result, the earth is impoverished and it yields less.

The stripping of trees from the landscape for fuel and charcoal production hastens desertification. Millions of acres of Africa's watersheds are being degraded, resulting in severe soil erosion. In Kenya, the charcoal sources for Nairobi have moved to the slopes of Mt. Kenya, more than 125 miles (200 km) away. Fuel wood sources for Mogadishu and Somalia are 300 miles (500 km) to the south. As people travel for sources of fuel, the areas they utilize are soon debased.

Meanwhile, soil erosion in Sudan, Ethiopia, and Tanzania often reaches 200 tons per acre (180 t per ha) per year. In all, three to seven million square miles (8 to 18 million square km) of sub-Saharan Africa are threatened by desertification.

People come to the Bunsura River in Nigeria in search of water. The arid landscape may yield nothing.

CURRENT TRENDS

Nomadism is vanishing as the land is increasingly swallowed by sand. Twenty years ago in the Sahelian nation of Mauritania, one out of two children were born in the desert. Sixty-five percent of the population were nomads; by 1976, that percentage had dropped by nearly half. As sand overtakes villages, the nomads drift south to shantytowns that are clapped together around Nouakchott, Mauritania's capital. Nouakchott's population has tripled since the nomads arrived. In 1987, the city was dubbed "the largest refugee camp in the world." The fiercely independent herdsmen, who once guided their cattle with pride, now huddle in shacks at the city's edge, afflicted with shame as well as hunger.

Drought is a familiar occurrence in the African ecosystem; for the past 2,500 years, dry spells have come and gone without extreme loss of human life, livestock, or crops. In Ethiopia, for example, a cycle of drought has been observed locally every year, regionally every three or four years, and on a widespread basis every eight to 10 years. While severe droughts have definitely triggered occasional food shortages in the past, recent dry spells have been exacerbated by overexploitation and mismanagement of a fragile resource base, with tragic results.

The current drought in the Sahel first struck in 1968. Up to 1973, at least 250,000 people and 3½ million cattle died. As farmers saw their grain production diminish by half, they were forced to eat their seeds, eliminating the following year's crop. The first of the migrations towards Nouakchott began. From 1974 to 1982, sparse and unevenly distributed rainfall descended on the Sahel. Then in 1983 and 1984, rainfall was the lowest recorded in this century, and a disastrous famine gripped Ethiopia. Millions of people, immobilized by hunger, filled the refugee camps. Almost $5 billion of emergency supplies and six million tons (5 million metric tons) of food were airlifted to the region. Between 1983 and 1985, from two to four million Africans died of starvation and disease. The rains returned 12 months later, and about half of the refugees left the camps. Yet 150 million people—almost one-quarter of Africa's population—remain hungry or malnourished.

The margin between what African soil will yield and how easily it is eroded is very fine. A decade of above-average rainfall in the 1950s led to a flurry of extensive cultivation of fallow and marginal areas. The very regions that were overfarmed—the Sahel, Ethiopia, Sudan, Somalia, and Mozambique—were the hardest hit by the famine in 1984.

From 1977 to 1987, over $10 billion was spent on aid throughout the Sahel with little beneficial effect. The desert continues to inexorably extend its domain; people are still being displaced; hunger is a daily scourge, and resources are dwindling. Obviously, a single solution, a "perfect" economic development scheme, or even a blueprint for African development is out of the question. Sub-Saharan Africa's more than 40 countries have varying cultural, economic, political, soil, climate, and ecological conditions. African ecosystems range from the hot, humid rain forests of the Congo River Basin to the highlands of Kenya, to the savannahs that grade into the Sahara Desert. Africa is simply too diverse to respond to monolithic solutions.

What has worked for Africa are multifaceted, locally applied approaches aimed at minimizing desertification. In Burkina Faso, less than 20 inches (50 cm) of rain fall each year. When the rains do come, they splash in torrents upon the baked earth, scooping it away. Nevertheless, a program of rainwater harvesting has induced the crusted soil to produce food.

Through an OXFAM project, women learned that they could improve the yield of their crops without using pesticides or machinery. They simply had to build lines of stones along a level contour of the land. Rain runs downhill until it meets the ridge of stones. The flow of water is slowed; soil and vegetable matter collect and water even seeps through the crusty top layer into the ground. Plants begin to take root. A year after the first wall was built, a crop of millet was harvested.

In other villages, desertification has caused wells to go dry. Inhabitants responded by enlarging a dam that captures rainwater running off a small hill. In 1986, the dam held water for three months. The villagers made it wider and higher so that it would store even more rain, which trickles into the ground and raises the water table. Their efforts were rewarded the following year, when their wells held a greater amount of water.

Goram Goram, a center of trade in the Sahel, was where a group of delegates from several different nomadic tribes met in 1987. These tribes were the main cattle herders in the region. They knew that too many cattle had overgrazed the land and turned it into desert, and agreed to persuade their people to breed smaller, higher-quality herds. This would ensure the same income, but less pasture would be devoured. Although the nomads face many obstacles—one of which is that they are not well represented in the government—they are striving to create guaranteed markets which will continue to make it worthwhile for them to raise cattle.

Although the cycle of desertification in the Sahel is proceeding faster than the strategy of replanting trees, there are indications elsewhere that abused land will be reclaimed. In West Africa, fragile soils are a limiting factor in the practice of intensive agriculture. But farmers have begun to use mulch or compost to reduce erosion and conserve the soil. A 10 percent slope planted with maize normally endured a rain runoff of 42 percent. With the addition of mulch, runoff was only 6 percent. Soil conservation was even more dramatic. Losses were decreased by 97 percent. Although desertification of the Sahel continues, public education and world attention are being focused on the issue. If recovery programs can be instituted, there is a chance that the Sahelians will once again subsist on their ancestral land.

A woman in Cameroon plants seedlings, hopeful for a harvest.

What Can Be Done?

On Cape Cod, dune erosion control is attempted.

Whether you've just learned what a CFC is, or are a seasoned environmental activist, it's hard not to feel overwhelmed by the facts in this book. You may be wondering, "What's the use? The pollution and destruction are too rampant to ever be halted."

It's not too late, however. You are alive in the 1990s, the "decade of the environment." The National Wildlife Federation claims that if you convinced two people to do something for the environment, and the next day *they* convinced two people, and so on, less than a month would pass before everyone in the United States would be alerted to take action. You can make a difference.

You have tremendous power as an individual. You can think. You can educate yourself about a situation, and then act accordingly.

It may be convenient to stop at a fast-food restaurant for a hamburger, but all of us will experience climatic changes from diminishing rain forests. You can make a decision not to consume fast food. The ivory trade causes 80,000 elephants a year to be slain for their tusks. If the slaughter continues, every wild elephant will be killed in less than five years—but we will have plenty of tie clasps and earrings to remember them by—unless you decide not to buy ivory.

Must destruction be the legacy of our species? Are humans incapable of appreciating the flora and fauna of a given ecosystem for their contributions to the entire scheme of life without profiting from the abuse of our resources?

We have exploited earth's resources for our comfort and vanity, regardless of the cost. Now, the fact that we haven't taken responsibility for our actions is catching up with us. It is reflected in the degraded state of our planet. If we don't immediately decide to live in a sustainable manner, nature will simply continue to make the decision for us—by providing a habitat less and less habitable.

To stop and think about a product before we buy it may seem like a loss of freedom, but it is the only way to ensure an acceptable quality of life for ourselves and future generations. You, your children, and their children deserve to see the ocean brimming with fish and seashells, not sewage and hypodermic needles. This means we have to think about what we buy and how we dispose of it.

You also have tremendous power as a consumer. Read labels. Can the package be recycled? Does the product contain harmful ingredients? Why spend money on products that will pollute the environment—and ourselves—as we use them? Take a moment to drop a postcard in the mail to the manufacturer saying why you didn't buy the product. Realize the power that you have to remove wasteful packaging and harmful products from the shelves simply by not buying them!

Appendix I contains specific suggestions for individual actions you can take to make a difference today. Appendices II and III list environmental organizations and sources of further information, respectively. Things *can* change if we think about what we are doing to the earth, the place where we live. Remember, we can talk about the ozone layer, and the ocean, and the rain forests. . . but in the end, the most endangered environments on the planet are our own bodies. We are at the top of the food chain. If what we consume is sick, we will be sick.

Every action we perform can be likened to a footstep on the earth; it will leave an imprint. Therefore, step lightly.

APPENDIX I: WHAT YOU CAN DO NOW TO HELP

© Michael Baytoff

THE OZONE LAYER

1. Avoid buying products packaged in polystyrene. Choose cardboard egg cartons. Although disposable products are wasteful always select paper instead of polystyrene.

2. If you eat at fast-food chains, patronize those offering biodegradable packaging. If you notice the restaurant's using foam cups, write to the chain headquarters and ask them to stop:

Robert L. Barney, Chief Executive Officer, Wendy's International
4228 W. Dublin Granville Rd.
Dublin, OH 43017

Jerry W. Levin, Chairman of the Board, Burger King Corp.
7360 N. Kendall Dr.
Miami, FL 33156

Richard P. Mayer, Chief Executive Officer, Kentucky Fried Chicken
P.O. Box 32070
Louisville, KY 40232

J. W. Marriott, Chief Executive Officer, Marriott Corp. (Roy Rogers)
10400 Fernwood Rd.
Bethesda, MD 20058

Fred Turner, Chairman of the Board, McDonald's Corp.
One McDonald Plaza
Oak Brook, IL 60521

3. Don't purchase CFC/halon products, such as:

- Halon fire extinguishers—dry chemical ones work just as well
- CFC dusting sprays
- CFC-propelled foam party streamers
- CFC noise horns
- CFC foam insulation—use fiberglass or cellulose

4. Ask store managers not to sell CFC/halon products.

5. Car air-conditioning tips:

- Service your car air conditioner at shops that recycle
- Ask shops to buy and use CFC-recycling equipment
- Each visit to the gas station, ask if they recycle CFCs
- Write a letter to your newspaper supporting shops that recycle CFCs
- Ask auto supply stores not to sell CFC coolant recharge cans

6. Find out if the business/industry where you work uses CFCs or halons. Inquire about opportunities to reduce usage.

7. Support local, state, and national initiatives to protect the ozone layer. Start a letter-writing campaign.

8. Contact your local Department of Environmental Protection about establishing a CFC-recycling program in your community.

9. Write to Friends of the Earth to request their booklet, *Ozone Protection Plan: Essential Elements* on the Ozone Campaign Action Alert:
Friends of the Earth
218 D St. S.E.
Washington, DC 20003

10. Write your government representatives. Ask them to support a CFC and halon phase-out, labeling of ozone-destroying products, and mandatory CFC recycling. One letter to a member of Congress can change a vote!
Address your mail to:
The Honorable ______________________
U.S. Senate OR U.S. House of Representatives
Washington, DC 20515

11. For freshening the air indoors, choose potpourri or plants over aerosol room fresheners. While new aerosols may not damage the ozone layer, many use isobutane and propane, substances that can harm your heart and nervous system. Plants cleanse the air in your house naturally. Philodendrons and gerbera daisies are most effective.

THE OCEAN

1. Remember, plastics are made from petroleum, a non-renewable resource. Even though photodegradeable plastic six-pack carriers are replacing non-degradeable carriers, they still allow the creation of more and more plastic and the continued use of oil. During the manufacture of plastics, five of the six chemicals ranked by the EPA as causing the most hazardous waste are produced. Push for product packaging that is not disposable, but can be used again, such as glass containers. Pressure manufacturers and legislators to leave the "disposable" mentality behind and begin non-wasteful packaging now!

2. Never dispose of toxic or hazardous chemicals in your septic system, down the sink, or on the ground. These contaminate groundwater supplies. Use non-toxic products to accomplish the same results.

3. Avoid using excess detergents or other chemicals in maintaining your boat. Use biodegradable products.

4. Recycle used motor oil at collection sites—don't dump it on the ground! A single quart of oil can contaminate thousands of gallons of ground water. Thirty percent of the oil in the ocean arrives from used oil dumped on the ground.

5. Use natural, non-toxic approaches to insect control whenever possible. Save dangerous materials such as pesticides for hazardous waste pick-up or recycling days in your community.

6. Don't buy balloons—they end up in the ocean and kill sea life. Encourage stores to be considerate of the environment when they are ordering party goods.

7. Buy phosphate-free soaps and detergents; ask your supermarket to carry them if they don't already.

8. Buy personal care products from companies that are environmentally conscious, such as The Body Shop. All ingredients are natural, derived from unthreatened sources. No products are tested on animals. Only recycled paper, and as little of that as possible, is used. Call (800) 541-2535 for a catalog printed on recycled paper.

9. Use natural substitutes for harmful drain and oven cleaners and toxic household chemicals. Five basic ingredients serve most household cleaning needs very well: baking soda, white vinegar, borax, biodegradable soaps, and washing soda. Write to Greenpeace for their comprehensive guide to substitutes for commonly-used chemicals, *Stepping Lightly on the Earth: Everyone's Guide to Toxics in the Home.*

10. Avoid buying tampons with plastic applicators. Consider switching from paper-based sanitary napkins and tampons (bleached white goods contain dioxin and often are irradiated for sterilization) to natural sea sponges, available in health stores.

11. For a kit about plastics legislation, lobbyists for the plastics industry, and alternatives to using plastic, contact:

Berkeley Ecology Center
1403 Addison St.
Berkeley, CA 94702
Or call: (415) 548-2220.

12. Take part in beach clean-ups. If you don't live near the ocean, be careful what you buy and how you dispose of it.

THE GREAT LAKES

1. Order the book *Great Lakes, Great Legacy* by Dr. Richard Liroff, or request it at your library. Copies are $20 + $2 postage. Order from:

The Conservation Foundation
P.O. Box 4866
Hampden Post Office, Baltimore, MD 21211
Or, call (301) 338-6951.
Canadian orders, please call (800) 565-0659.

2. Educate yourself about the toxins in your environment. Subscribe to the weekly newsletter "Rachel's Hazardous Waste News," edited by Dr. Peter Montague. Subscription rates are $8 for students and seniors, $25 for individuals/groups. Write to:

Environmental Research Foundation
P.O. Box 3541
Princeton, NJ 08543

3. Contact Paul Bierman-Lytle, who designs non-toxic homes, from paints to plywood. He resides in Connecticut. Call: (203) 966-3541.

4. Become an environmental shopper. This booklet for $2, including postage, tells you how. Write in care of "Environmental Shopping." Make checks payable to:

Pennsylvania Resource Council, P.O. Box 88, Media, PA 19063

5. Join Work on Waste U.S.A. to learn about incineration in the Great Lakes, nationwide and worldwide. Weekly newsletter costs $50 per year. Order *Waste Management As If the Future Mattered*, a 48-page booklet, for $3 each, or $2 each for orders over 10 copies. (Get the neighbors involved.) Write to:

Work on Waste U.S.A.
82 Judson St.
Canton, NY 13617

A thrilling video by the same name ($30) can be ordered from:

Video-Active Productions
Box 322, Route 2
Canton, NY 13617

6. An eye-opening book on composting is *Worms Eat My Garbage*, available with other composting-related products from:

The Philadelphia Worm Company
P.O. Box 9580
Philadelphia, PA 19124

7. Substitute natural cedar blocks, renewed by sanding, for moth balls in clothing drawers. A dozen blocks cost $11.98 from The Lillian Vernon catalog. Call (914) 633-6300 for mail order. (Inquire where the cedar is obtained from; are rain forest woods being depleted?)

8. The Department of Natural Resources publishes a pamphlet on "Hazardous Waste in Your Home: Here's What You Should Do!" To get one, write to:

Wisconsin DNR
Bureau of Water Resources Management
Box 7921
Madison, WI 53707

9. Request "Toward a Chlorine-Free Paper Industry" from Greenpeace. Then, express your preference for buying and using low-bleach or no-bleach products at the supermarket, area businesses, your workplace and at local paper distributors. To learn more about encouraging policy changes at individual mills at the state and federal level, contact:

Shelley Stewart, Greenpeace
4649 Sunnyside Ave. N.
Seattle, WA 98103

Renate Kroesa, Greenpeace
2623 W. 4th Ave.
Vancouver, BC Canada V6K 1P8

10. For organic lawn and garden care, contact:

Ringer Company
9959 Valley View Rd.
Minneapolis, MN 55344
Or call: (800) 654-1047.

THE TROPICAL RAIN FORESTS

1. Learn about a global reforestation program sponsored by the American Forestry Association. Write them at:

"Global Re-Leaf," P.O. Box 2000
Washington, DC 20013

2. Barlow Tyrie, makers of garden furniture, switched to plantation wood from Java rather than deplete natural teak forests. Call them with thanks or order a catalog at (800) 451-7467.

3. Avoid buying new furniture or products made with tropical forest woods. Let the manufacturers and furniture showrooms know why you are not buying them. Common woods are:

- Mahogany (West Indies, West Coast of Africa)
- Teak (Southeast Asia)
- Rosewood (Brazil)
- Ebony (Africa, India, Sri Lanka)
- Ramin (Southeast Asia)
- Afromose (Africa)
- Iroko (Africa)
- Cedar (Central and South America, as well as the U.S. and Canada)

Carpenters and building contractors, don't buy plywood made from timber clear-cut from rain forests!

4. Write for the Tropical Rain Forest Information Packet ($5) from:

Institute for Gaean Economics
64 Main St.
Montpelier, VT 05602

5. Boycott products made by companies that destroy the rain forests. Write and tell them! Here is a partial list:

- Kimberly Clark Corporation
  P.O. Box 619100
  DFW Airport Station
  Dallas, TX 75261
  Countries: Colombia, El Salvador, Mexico. Products: "Hi-Dri" paper towels, "Delsey," "Huggies" disposable diapers, "Kotex," "Light Days," "New Freedom," "Depend" incontinence products.

- Georgia-Pacific Corporation
  133 Peachtree St. N.E.
  Atlanta, GA 30303
  Countries: Indonesia, Philippines (The Philippines has only 5 percent of its forest left.) Products: "Coronet," "Mr. Big," "Delta," "M-D tissues/paper towels, containers, packaging, specialty products."

- RJR Nabisco, Inc.
  300 Galleria Parkway
  Atlanta, GA 30339
  Country: plantations in Honduras. Products: "Del Monte," "Hawaiian Punch," "Ortega," "College Inn" soups, "Planters," "Milk-Bone" dog biscuits, all "Nabisco" brand foods, "Fleischmann's" and "Blue Bonnet" margarines, "Dromedary," plus alcohol and tobacco products.

- Castle & Cooke, Inc.
  10900 Wilshire Blvd.
  Los Angeles, CA 90024
  Country: plantations in Honduras. Products: "Dole" brand, "Bud of California" produce, "Figaro" cat food.

6. For $5 per tree, you can "adopt" a seedling in Costa Rica and help save the rain forests. For $250, you will re-forest a full hectare—about 1000 trees. Write:
The Basic Foundation
P.O. Box 47012
St. Petersburg, FL 33743

7. Boycott fast-food hamburger and processed beef products. Two-thirds of the rain forests in Central America have been cleared to raise a poor grade of cattle. The United States imports 130 million pounds of fresh and frozen beef from these countries every year for the fast-food market.

8. Pesticides banned in the United States, Europe, and Canada are sent to Third World countries for use in export agriculture. In Peru, cocoa plants are being eradicated near the Amazon headwaters. The U.S. State Department is using highly toxic herbicides that are killing rare rain forest plants and animals downstream, poisoning rivers and contaminating topsoil. These cancer-causing pesticides end up back in the United States on the food we import. Write to your Senator or Congressional representative to help break the "circle of poison."

9. Send a letter to the president of the World Bank urging him to stop financing rain forest dams that drown thousands of acres of rain forests, displace indigenous tribes, and saddle developing countries with a permanent mountain of debt. Ask him to fund small-scale projects that benefit rain forests and their inhabitants instead. Write to:
Mr. Barber J. Conable, Jr., President
World Bank
1818 H St. N.W.
Washington, DC 20433

10. NASA satellites spotted 170,000 fires last year in the Brazilian province of Rondonia, a rich ecosystem that has lost 20 percent of its rain forest. The burning of rain forests accounts for a significant portion of the global output of carbon dioxide, the main cause of the greenhouse effect. Send a letter to the General Secretary of the U.N. Environment Programme, asking for an emergency session to plan global action to douse the Amazon fires. Write to:
Mostafa Kamal Tolba, Executive Director
U.N. Environment Programme
P.O. Box 30552
Nairobi, Kenya

DESERTIFICATION

1. Subscribe to "Earth Ethics." This quarterly publication focuses on evolving values for an Earth community. Subscription by contribution. Write to:
Public Resource Foundation
1815 H Street N.W., Suite 600
Washington, DC 20006

2. For information on soil erosion, write to:
Earthsave
706 Frederick St.
Santa Cruz, CA 95062-2205

3. Encourage your legislators to focus on the research and development of organic farming, along with economic and educational incentives to help farmers end the use of hazardous chemicals.

4. Consider how production of your food affects the environment. Animals raised for food in the United States eat enough grain to feed more than five times the U.S. population; if Americans reduced meat-eating by 10 percent, the 12 million tons of grain saved annually could feed all the people on earth who starve to death. Animal agriculture is responsible for 85 percent of topsoil loss, 260 million acres of forest destruction, over half our water consumption, 20 billion pounds of manure every day that contaminate our ground water, and 25 times the fossil fuel needed to produce the same amount of protein in grain. Eat lower on the food chain—vegetables, fruits, grains; decrease consumption of meat and animal products for ethical reasons as well. Encourage restaurants to serve vegetarian dishes. For information on factory farming, read *Animal Liberation* by Peter Singer, Avon Books, 1975. Contact:
The Humane Farming Association
1550 California St., Suite 10
San Francisco, CA 94109
Or call: (415) 771-2253.

5. Support laws that ban harmful pesticides and that require disclosure of pesticides, drugs, and other chemicals used in food production; support markets that offer contaminant-free food.

6. Buy organic food, locally grown if possible. Encourage your market to stock locally-grown produce. Support family farming.

7. Inform schools, hospitals, airlines, and media of your food concerns.

8. Educate yourself about the loss of topsoil worldwide through harmful farming practices. "Acres U.S.A." highlights eco-agriculture. A subscription costs $15 per year from:

Acres U.S.A.
10008 E. 60th Terrace
Kansas City, MO 64133

9. Save trees! Use cloth napkins instead of paper, rags instead of paper towels, mugs instead of paper cups.

10. Ask for recycled paper at stationery shops and printing stores.

APPENDIX II: ENVIRONMENTAL ORGANIZATIONS

© Rob Mustard

UNITED STATES

ALABAMA

Alabama Wildlife Foundation
46 Commerce St.
P.O. Box 2102
Montgomery 36102
(205) 832-9453

The Alabama Conservancy
2717 7th Ave. South
Suite 201
Birmingham 35233
(205) 322-3126

ALASKA

North American Wolf Society
P.O. Box 82950
Fairbanks 99708

Trustees for Alaska
725 Christensen Dr.
Suite #4
Anchorage 99501
(907) 276-4244

Prince William Sound Renewal Project
2270 Fritz Cove Rd.
Juneau 99801
(907) 789-5683

ARIZONA

Arizona Conservation Council
Box 11312
Phoenix 85061

Arizona Wildlife Federation
4330 N. 62nd St.
#102
Scottsdale 85251
(602) 946-6160

ARKANSAS

The Ozark Society
P.O. Box 2914
Little Rock 72203

Arkansas Wildlife Federation
7509 Cantrell Rd.
#226
Little Rock 72207
(501) 663-7255

CALIFORNIA

American Cetacean Society
P.O. Box 2639
San Pedro, CA 90731-0943
(213) 548-6279

Save the Dolphins Project
Earth Island Institute
300 Broadway
Suite 28
San Francisco 94133
(415) 788-3666/1-800-3-DOLFIN

Save the Redwoods League
114 Sansome St.
Rm. #605
San Francisco 94104
(415) 362-2352

California Wildlife Defenders
P.O. Box 2025
Hollywood 90078
(213) 663-1856

Friends of the Sea Otter
P.O. Box 221220
Carmel 93922
(408) 625-6965

Coalition for Clean Air
309 Santa Monica Blvd.
Suite 212
Santa Monica 90401
(213) 451-0651

Northcoast Environmental Center
879 Ninth St.
Arcata 95521
(707) 822-6918

Save San Francisco Bay Association
P.O. Box 925
Berkeley 94701
(415) 849-3053

Treepeople
12601 Mulholland Dr.
Beverly Hills 90210
(818) 753-4600

COLORADO

The American Humane Association
9725 E. Hampden
Denver 80231
(303) 695-0811

Colorado Water Congress
1390 Logan St.
Suite 312
Denver 80203
(303) 837-0812

CONNECTICUT

Long Island Sound Taskforce of the Oceanic Society
Stamford Marine Center
Magee Ave.
Stamford 06902
(203) 327-9786

Audubon Council of Connecticut
Rt. 4
Box 171
Sharon 06069
(203) 364-0520

DELAWARE

Forward Lands, Inc.
2800 Pennsylvania Ave.
Wilmington 19806
(302) 655-2151

The Delaware Nature Society
Box 700
Hockessin 19707
(302) 239-2334

DISTRICT OF COLUMBIA

Marine Mammal Commission
1625 I St. N.W.
Washington, DC 20006
(202) 653-6237

American Horse Protection Association, Inc.
1000 29th St. N.W.
Suite T-100
Washington, DC 20007
(202) 965-0500

Committee for Conservation and Care of Chimpanzees
3819 48th St.
Washington, DC 20016
(202) 362-1993

Defenders of Wildlife
1244 19th St. N.W.
Washington, DC 20036
(202) 659-9510

The Humane Society of the United States
2100 L St. N.W.
Washington, DC 20037
(202) 452-1100

National Geographic Society
17th & M Sts. N.W.
Washington, DC 20036
(202) 857-7000

Society for Animal Protective Legislation
P.O. Box 3719
Georgetown Station
Washington, DC 20007
(202) 337-2334

FLORIDA

Save the Manatee Club
500 N. Maitland Ave.
Maitland 32751
(407) 539-0990

Florida Public Interest Research Group
308 E. Park Ave.
Suite 213
Tallahassee 32301
(904) 224-5304

Florida Defenders of the Environment, Inc.
Home Office
1523 N.W. 4th St.
Gainesville 32601
(904) 372-6965

GEORGIA

The Georgia Conservancy, Inc.
781 Marietta St. N.W.
Atlanta 30318
(404) 872-8200

Georgia Environmental Council
P.O. Box 2388
Decatur 30031-2388
(404) 262-1967

HAWAII

Life of the Land
19 Niolopa Pl.
Honolulu 96817
(808) 595-3903

The Outdoor Circle
200 N. Vineyard Blvd.
#506
Honolulu 96817
(808) 521-0074

IDAHO

The Peregrine Fund, Inc.
5666 West Flying Hawk Ln.
Boise 83709
(208) 362-3716

Idaho Wildlife Federation
Rt. 3
Centro Dr.
Twin Falls 83301
(208) 733-7111

ILLINOIS

The Eagle Foundation, Inc.
300 E. Hickory St.
Apple River 61001
(815) 594-2259

Illinois Natural Heritage Foundation
320 S. 3rd St.
Rockford 61104
(815) 964-6666

Open Lands Project
220 S. State St.
Suite 1880
Chicago 60604
(312) 427-4256

Illinois Audubon Society
P.O. Box 608
Wayne 60184
(312) 584-6290

INDIANA

Acres, Inc.
1802 Chapman Rd.
P.O. Box 141
Huntertown 46748
(219) 637-6264

Association of Great Lakes Outdoor Writers
301 Cross St.
Sullivan 47882
(812) 268-6232

IOWA

Iowa Ornithologists' Union
845 Cypress Ct.
Iowa City 52245

Iowa Natural Heritage Foundation
Insurance Exchange Bldg.
Suite 1005
505 Fifth Ave.
Des Moines 50309
(515) 288-1846

KANSAS

Wildlife Society Kansas Chapter
Bob Culbertson, Pres.
P.O. Box 582
New Strawn 66839
(316) 364-2282

Kansas Ornithological Society
Elmer J. Finck
Division of Biology
Kansas State University
Manhattan 66506
(913) 532-6629

KENTUCKY

American Cave Conservation Association
131 Main & Cave Sts.
P.O. Box 409
Horse Cave 42749
(502) 786-1466

Kentucky Resources Council
P.O. Box 1070
Frankfort 40602
(502) 875-2428

LOUISIANA

Elsa Wild Animal Appeal
Louisiana Chapter
Laura Lanza
1540 Chateau Cir.
Lake Charles 70605
(318) 477-9782

MAINE

Eagle Hill Wildlife Research Station
Steuben 04680
(207) 546-2821

Maine Coast Heritage Trust
167 Park Row
Brunswick 04011
(207) 729-7366

MARYLAND

North American Bluebird Society
P.O. Box 6295
Silver Spring 20906
(301) 384-2798

Rachel Carson Council, Inc.
8940 Jones Mill Rd.
Chevy Chase 20815
(301) 652-1877

Committee to Preserve Assateague Island, Inc.
616 Piccadilly Rd.
Towson 21204
(301) 828-4520

MASSACHUSETTS

Union of Concerned Scientists
26 Church St.
Cambridge 02238
(617) 547-5552

Conservation Law Foundation of New England
3 Joy St.
Boston 02108
(617) 742-2540

Woods Hole Oceanographic Institute
Woods Hole 02543
(617) 548-1400

MICHIGAN

Michigan Nature Association
7981 Beard Rd.
Box 102
Avoca 48006
(313) 324-2626

West Michigan Environmental Action Council
1432 Wealthy S.E.
Grand Rapids 49506
(616) 451-3051

MINNESOTA

Friends of Animals and Their Environment
P.O. Box 7283
Minneapolis 55407

Minnesota Herpetological Society
James Ford Bell Museum of Natural History
10 Church St. S.E.
University of Minnesota
Minneapolis 55455-0104
(612) 626-2031

Friends of the Boundary Waters Wilderness
1313 5th St. S.E.
Suite 329
Minneapolis 55414
(612) 379-3835

MISSISSIPPI

Gulf Coast Research Laboratory
Ocean Springs 39564
(601) 875-2244

Mississippi Wildlife Federation
520 North President St.
Jackson 39201
(601) 353-6922

MISSOURI

Missouri Prairie Foundation
P.O. Box 200
Columbia 65205

Conservation Federation of Missouri
728 W. Main St.
Jefferson City, 65101-1543
(314) 634-2322

MONTANA

Northern Rockies Action Group, Inc.
9 Placer St.
Helena 59601
(406) 442-6615

Montana Land Reliance
P.O. Box 355
Helena 59625
(406) 443-7027

NEBRASKA

Izaak Walton League of America, Inc.
Nebraska Div.
Delmer Miller, Pres.
4828 J St.
Lincoln 68510
(402) 488-1640

NEVADA

Nevada Wildlife Federation
P.O. Box 71238
Reno 89570
(702) 825-5158

NEW HAMPSHIRE

Elm Research Institute
Harrisville 03450
(1-800-FOR-ELMS)

Seacoast Anti-Pollution League
5 Market St.
Portsmouth
(603) 431-5089

NEW JERSEY

American Littoral Society
Sandy Hook
Highlands 07732
(201) 291-0055

Cause for Concern
R.D. #1
Box 570
Stewartsville 08886
(201) 479-6778

Genesis Farm, Ecological Learning Center
P.O. Box 607
Blairstown 07825
(201) 362-6735

Food & Water, Inc.
3 Whitman Dr.
Denville 07834
(201) 625-3111

Grass Roots Environmental Organization
Box 2018
Bloomfield 07003
(201) 429-8965

Environmental Response Network
P.O. Box 105
Ocean View 08230
(609) 861-0090

State Coalition Against Incineration
19 Girard Pl.
Maplewood 07040
(201) 762-4912

Save Our Oceans
160 Pershing Blvd.
Lavallette 08735
(201) 793-5253

NEW MEXICO

New Mexico Wildlife Federation
3240-D Juan Tabo N.E.
Suite 10
Albuquerque 87111
(505) 299-5404

NEW YORK

Food and Water, Inc.
225 Lafayette St.
Room 612
New York City 10012
(212) 941-9340

Fund for Animals
40 W. 57th St.
New York City 10019
(212) 246-2096

National Audubon Society
950 Third Ave.
New York City 10022
(212) 832-3200

Institute of Ecosystem Study
The New York Botanical Garden
Mary Flagler Cary Arboretum
Box AB
Millbrook 12545
(914) 677-5343

Scenic Hudson, Inc.
9 Vassar St.
Poughkeepsie 12601
(914) 473-4440

Work on Waste U.S.A.
82 Judson St.
Canton 13617
(315) 379-9200

NORTH CAROLINA

North Carolina Coastal Federation
1832 J. Bell Lane
New Port 28570
(919) 393-8185

The Acid Rain Foundation, Inc.
1410 Varsity Dr.
Raleigh 27606
(919) 828-9443

Carolina Bird Club, Inc.
P.O. Box 27647
Raleigh 27611

North Carolina Herpetelogical Society
John Wiley, Pediatrics/Genetics
3N51
East Carolina University School of Medicine
Greenville 27834
(919) 551-2530

NORTH DAKOTA

North Dakota Natural Science Society
P.O. Box 8238
University Station
Grand Forks
58202-8238
(701) 777-2199

OHIO

The Committee for National Arbor Day
Mrs. Edward H. Scanlon
Honorary National Chairwoman
P.O. Box 38247
Olmstead Falls 44138

The Dawes Arboretum
7770 Jacksontown Rd. S.E.
Newark 43055
(614) 323-2355

OKLAHOMA

Oklahoma Wildlife Federation
4545 Lincoln Blvd.
Suite 171
Oklahoma City 73105
(405) 524-7009

OREGON

Oregon State Public Interest Research Group
027 S.W. Arthur
Portland 97201
(503) 222-9641

PENNSYLVANIA

S.A.V.E.
P.O. Box 26
Coopersburg 18036
(215) 282-2364

Wildlands Conservancy
601 Orchid Place
Emmaus 18049-1637
(215) 965-4397

RHODE ISLAND

Save The Bay, Inc.
434 Smith St.
Providence 02908-3732
(401) 272-3540

Audubon Society of Rhode Island
12 Sanderson Rd.
Smithfield 02911
(401) 231-6444

SOUTH CAROLINA

International Primate Protection League
P.O. Box 766
Summerville 29484
(803) 871-2280

SOUTH DAKOTA

South Dakota Resources Coalition
P.O. Box 7020
Brookings 57007
(605) 594-3558

TENNESSEE

National Foundation to Protect America's Eagles
P.O. Box 120206
Nashville 37212
(615) 847-4171

Tennessee Environmental Council
1725 Church St.
Nashville 37203
(615) 321-5075

TEXAS

Bat Conservation International
P.O. Box 162603
Austin 78716
(512) 327-9721

Native Plant Society of Texas
P.O. Box 891
Georgetown 78627
(214) 327-6220

Waterfowl Habitat Alliance of Texas
1973 West Gray
Suite 6
Houston 77019
(713) 522-5025

UTAH

Utah Nature Study Society
Maria Dickerson, Sec'y.
323 S. 2nd West
Tooele 84074

VERMONT

Vermont Audubon Council
Abbott Fenn, Pres.
P.O. Box 521
Middlebury 05753
(802) 545-2538

Vermont Institute of Natural Science
Church Hill Rd.
Woodstock 05091
(802) 457-2779

VIRGINIA

Citizens Clearinghouse for Hazardous Waste
P.O. Box 926
Arlington 22216
(703) 276-7070

The Izaak Walton League of America, Inc.
1401 Wilson Blvd.
Level B
Arlington 22209
(703) 528-1818

WASHINGTON

Friends of the Earth
4512 University Way N.E.
Seattle 98105
(206) 633-1661

Children of the Green Earth
Box 95219
Seattle 98145

Washington Wildlife Heritage Foundation
32610 Pacific Hwy. S.
Federal Way 98003
(206) 874-1800

WEST VIRGINIA

Brooks Nature Center
Oglebay Institute
Oglebay Park
Wheeling 26003
(304) 242-6855

West Virginia Highlands Conservancy
P.O. Box 306
Charleston 25321

WISCONSIN

Trees for Tomorrow, Inc.
611 Sheridan Rd.
Box 609
Eagle River 54521
(715) 479-6456/6457

Wetlands for Wildlife, Inc.
P.O. Box 344
West Bend 53095

The Wisconsin Society for Ornithology, Inc.
John H. Idzikowski
2558 South Delaware
Milwaukee 53207
(414) 744-4818

WYOMING

Powder River Basin Resource Council
P.O. Box 1178
Douglas 82633
(307) 358-5002

Wyoming Outdoor Council, Inc.
201 Main St.
Lander 82520
(307) 332-7031

AUSTRALIA

World Wildlife Fund Australia
Level 17, St. Martin's Towers
31 Market St.
G.P.O. Box S28
Sydney
NSW 2001

Friends of the Earth
P.O. Box A474
Sydney South
NSW 2000

Greenpeace Australia Ltd.
4th Floor
134 Broadway
NSW 2007

Greenpeace Australia Ltd.
P.O. Box 51
Balmair
NSW 2041

Australian Conservation Foundation
340 Gore St.
Fitzroy 3065
Victoria

The Rainforest Information Centre
P.O. Box 368
Lismore
NSW 2480

Rainforest Action Group
7 Wotherspoon St.
North Lismore
NSW 2480

The Wilderness Society
130 Davey St.
Hobart
TAS 7000

Friends of the Earth
4th floor
56 Foster St.
Surry Hills
NSW 2010

CANADA

Canadian Nature Federation
453 Sussex Dr.
Ottawa, ON K1N 6Z4
(613) 238-6154

Greenpeace Toronto
578 Bloor St. West
Toronto, ON M6G 1K1

Greenpeace Vancouver
2623 West 4th Ave.
Vancouver, B.C. V6K 1P8

World Wildlife Fund Canada
60 St. Clair Ave. East
Suite 201
Toronto, ON M4T 1M5

Alberta Wilderness Association
Box 6398
Station D
Calgary, AB T2P 2E1

Federation of Alberta Naturalists
Box 1472
Edmonton, AB T5J 2N5

Manitoba Naturalists Society
302-128 James Ave.
Winnipeg, MN R3B 0N8

Federation of British Columbia Naturalists
1200 Hornby St.
Vancouver, B.C. V6Z 2E2

New Brunswick Wildlife Federation
190 Cameron St.
Moncton, N.B. E1C 5Z2

Nova Scotia Wildlife Federation
P.O. Box 654
Halifax, N.S. B3J 2T3

Niagara Escarpment Commission
232 Guelph St.
Georgetown, ON L7G 4B1

Algonquin Wildlands League
229 College St.
Suite 206
Toronto, ON M5T 1R4

Jack Miner Migratory Bird Foundation, Inc.
P.O. Box 39
Kingsville, ON N9Y 2E8

Federation of Ontario Naturalists
355 Lesmill Rd.
Don Mills, ON M3B 2W8

Prince Edward Island Wildlife Federation
P.O. Box 190
Winsloe, P.E.I. C0A 2H0

Quebec Wildlife Federation
319 Est, Rue St.-Zotique
Montreal, P.Q. H2S 1L5

Province of Quebec Society for the Protection of Birds, Inc.
4832 de Maisonneuve Blvd. West
Montreal, P.Q. H3Z 1M5

Quebec Forestry Association, Inc.
Association Forestiere Quebecoise, Inc.
110, 915 St. Cyrille Blvd. West
Quebec City, P.Q. G1S 1T8

Saskatchewan Natural History Society
Box 414
Raymore, SK S0A 3J0

Saskatchewan Wildlife Federation
Box 788
Moose Jaw, SK S6H 4P5

Canadian Parks and Wilderness Society
69 Sherbourne St.
Suite 313
Toronto, ON M5A 3X7
(416) 366-3494

Canadian Forestry Association
185 Somerset St. West
Suite 203
Ottawa, ON K2P OJ2

Canadian Wildlife Federation
1673 Carling Ave.
Ottawa, ON K2A 3Z1
(613) 725-2191

Nature Conservancy of Canada
794A Broadview Ave.
Toronto, ON M4K 2P7
(416) 469-1701

Pollution Probe Foundation
12 Madison Ave.
Toronto, ON M5R 2S1
(416) 926-1907

Ontario Shade Tree Council
Attn Eric C. Oakleaf, Exec. Director
5 Shoreham Dr.
North York, ON M3N 1S4
(416) 661-6600

Canadian Federation of Humane Societies
30 Concourse Gate
Suite 102
Nepean, ON K2E 7V7

Wildlife Habitat Canada
1704 Carling Ave.
Suite 301
Ottawa, ON K2A 1C7
(613) 722-2090

APPENDIX III: SOURCES OF FURTHER INFORMATION

To find out more information about the environments presented in this book, contact the following organizations:

© Midgley/GreenPeace

THE OZONE LAYER

Friends of the Earth
218 D Street S.E.
Washington, DC 20003
(202) 544-2600

Worldwatch Institute
1776 Massachusetts Ave. N.W.
Washington, DC 20036
(202) 452-1999

Environmental Defense Fund
257 Park Ave.
New York, NY 10001
(212) 505-2100

Natural Resources Defense Council
Dept. #9
1350 New York Ave. N.W.
Washington, D.C. 20005
(202) 783-7800

Pollution Probe Foundation
12 Madison Ave.
Toronto, ON M5R 2S1
(416) 926-1907

Friends of the Earth
P.O. Box A474
Sydney South
NSW 2000

THE OCEAN

The Cousteau Society
930 W. 21st St.
Norfolk, Va. 23517
(804) 627-1144

Fondation Cousteau
25 Ave. Wagram
F75017 Paris, France
4766 0246

Greenpeace
P.O. Box 104432
Anchorage, AK 99510
(907) 277-8234

Prince William Sound Renewal Project
2270 Fritz Cove Rd.
Juneau, AK, 99801
(907) 789-5683

Greenpeace Vancouver
2623 West 4th Ave.
Vancouver, B.C. V6K 1P8
(604) 736-0321

National Ocean Sanctuary Coordinating Committee
P.O. Box 498
Mendocino, CA 95460
(707) 937-0700

Save Our Ocean Committee
160 Pershing Blvd.
Lavallette, NJ 08735
(201) 793-5253

Greenpeace Australia
4th Floor
134 Broadway
NSW 2007
(02) 555 7044

THE GREAT LAKES

Citizens for a Better Environment
647 W. Virginia St.
Suite 303
Milwaukee, WI 53204
(414) 271-7475

National Wildlife Federation's Great Lakes Natural Resource Center
802 Monroe
Ann Arbor, MI 48104
(313) 769-3351

Council of Great Lakes Governors
10th floor
310 S. Michigan Ave.
Chicago, IL 60604
(312) 427-0092

International Joint Commission
P.O. Box 32869
Detroit, Michigan 48232
(313) 226-2170
AND
International Joint Commission
Great Lakes Regional Office, Information Services
100 Ouellette Ave.
8th floor
Windsor, Ontario
N9A 673 Canada

The Pollution Probe Foundation
12 Madison Ave.
Toronto, Ontario
M5R 2S1 Canada
(416) 926-1907

The Sierra Club, Midwest Office
214 N. Henry St.
Suite 203
Madison, WI 53703
(608) 257-4994

Lake Erie Clean-Up Committee
3568 Brewster Rd.
Dearborn, MI 48120
(313) 271-8906

Greenpeace
921 W. Van Buren St.
Chicago, IL 60607
(312) 666-3305

Greenpeace
C.P. 151 Succursale De Lorimier
Montreal, PQ
H2H 2N6 Canada
(514) 274-5559

Greenpeace
427 Bloor St.
West, Toronto, Ontario
M55 1X7 Canada
(416) 922-3011

THE TROPICAL RAIN FORESTS

Rainforest Action Network
300 Broadway
San Francisco, CA 94133
(415) 398-4404

Rainforest Alliance
295 Madison Ave.
Suite 1804
New York, NY 10017
(212) 941-1900

Institute for Gaean Economics
64 Main St.
Montpelier, VT 05602

Rainforest Action Group
7 Wotherspoon St.
North Lismore
NSW 2480
(066) 21 8505

Children of the Green Earth
Box 95219
Seattle, WA 98145
(206) 781-0852

THE AFRICAN SAHEL

International Alliance for Sustainable Agriculture
1701 University Ave., S.E.
Room 202
Minneapolis, MN 54414
(612) 331-1099

International Erosion Control Association
P.O. Box 4904
Steamboat Springs, CO 80477
(303) 879-3010

International Union for Conservation of Nature
Regional Office Eastern Africa
P.O. Box 68200
Nairobi, Kenya
(002 542) 50 26 50/51

IUCN Regional Office Western Africa
B.P. 3215
Dakar, Senegal
(00221) 32 05 45

FURTHER READING

Abrahamson, Dean Edwin. *The Challenge of Global Warming*, Washington, DC: Island Press, 1989

Brown, Lester R., Alan Durning, Christopher Flavin, Lori Heise, Jodi Jacobson, Sandra Postel, Michael Renner, Cynthia Pollock Shea, Linda Starke. *State of the World 1989*, New York: W. W. Norton, 1989

Bulloch, David K. *The Wasted Ocean*, New York, Lyons and Burford, 1989

Cousteau, Jacques-Yves. *The Cousteau Almanac: An Inventory of Life on Our Water Planet*, Garden City, New York: Doubleday, 1981

Keefe, John and Pierce, Neal R. *The Great Lakes States of America*, New York: W. W. Norton, 1980

Miller, Jr., G. Tyler. *Living in the Environment*, Belmont, California: Wadsworth Publishing, 1982

O'Hara, Kathryn J., Suzanne Indicello, Rose Bierce. *A Citizen's Guide to Plastics in the Ocean*, Washington, DC: Center for Marine Conservation, 1988

Page, Jake. *Arid Lands*, Alexandria, Virginia: Time-Life Books, 1984

Sierra Club, Great Lakes United, Lake Michigan Federation, Citizens for a Better Environment. *Sweet Water, Bitter Rain: Toxic Air Pollution in the Great Lakes*, November, 1989

Whitaker, Jennifer S. *How Can Africa Survive?* New York: Harper and Row, 1988

INDEX